Historical Association Studies

The Vikings in Britain

Historical Association Studies

General Editors: Muriel Chamberlain and H. T. Dickinson

The Historical Association, founded in 1906, brings together people who share an interest in, and love for, the past. It aims to further the study and teaching of history at all levels: teacher and student, amateur and professional. This is one of over 100 publications available at preferential rates to members. Membership also includes journals at generous discounts and gives access to courses, conferences, tours and regional and local activities. Full details are available from The Secretary, The Historical Association, 59a Kennington Park Road, London SE11 4JH, telephone: 071-735 3901.

⏌ning hours: ⏋

Term-time opening ho

Mon, Tues. Thu
Wed

The Vikings in Britain

Henry Loyn

BLACKWELL
Oxford UK & Cambridge USA

First published 1994
First published in USA 1995

Blackwell Publishers
108 Cowley Road, Oxford, OX4 1JF, UK

238 Main Street
Cambridge, Massachusetts 02142 USA

British Library Cataloguing in Publication Data
A CIP catalogue record for this book is available from the British Library.

Library of Congress Cataloging-in-Publication Data has been applied for

ISBN 0–631–18711–1
ISBN 0–631–18712–X(pb)

Typeset in 10 on 12 pt English Times
by Colset Private Ltd, Singapore
Printed in Great Britain by Hartnolls Ltd, Bodmin

This book is printed on acid-free paper.

For Pat

Contents

Preface

Some years ago, I wrote on the subject of the Vikings in a book published by Batsford in 1977. In the intervening years there have been significant advances in the knowledge of the Viking world, and the bibliography, though short, attempts to bring to the English-speaking readers the most significant studies to have appeared during that period. The text has been compressed to conform to the needs of the Blackwell series, and some sections completely rewritten. The structure of argument remains much as before, to reveal the English experience in full British and Irish context and to interpret the early stages of Danish settlement in England as a significant migration.

Acknowledgements

Advances in scholarship in many disciplines have made it increasingly difficult to keep in touch with current discovery and thought among archaeologists, place-name specialists, numismatists and students of comparative institutions and societies, all of whom have contributed to a better understanding of the Viking impact and Scandinavian settlements in Britain. I wish to acknowledge here my indebtedness to my colleagues, notably those from the English Place-Name Society and the Society for Medieval Archaeology, and especially to the late Professor Michael Dolley for his help with numismatic problems and the late Dr Justin Schove for help with matters relating to climatic change. My thanks also go to Blackwell, and to their anonymous reader who saved me from several errors and infelicities. My greatest debt is to my wife to whom the book is formally dedicated.

H. R. L.

Maps

1

The Scandinavian world and Europe in the early Viking Age

The making of modern Europe was a slow and laborious business which the historian simplifies at peril. Modern conceptions of national growth and of national types are too easily applied to situations in the past where they are distorting, anachronistic and positively misleading. To be obsessed with the image of peaceful and peace-loving Scandinavian farmers, taken from the history of Scandinavia over the last two centuries, can lead to falsification as great as that provoked by the nursery and early schoolboy image of ruthless Viking axemen, horn-helmeted and heathen, breakers of skulls and despoilers of churches. Reality was much more complex. Not all farmers love peace. A ravager in May can turn a skilful hand to corn-harvest in August. One of the main objects of this book is to point to the highly complex human situation of raid and settlement, of piracy and cultivation that we mask under the conveniently smooth description of the Viking Age.

This Viking Age with its rough chronological extent from 800 to 1100 had a tremendous effect on the making of modern Europe. The process of recovery from the economic dislocation and political disaster which attended the fall of the Roman Empire in the West was not far advanced when the fresh wave of barbarian invasion struck. The historian, and especially the social and economic historian with his knowledge of happenings still to come, can see that this recovery was more than recovery, that Europe was proliferating in new growth, that the Carolingian world was different from and in many ways superior to the late Classical world it aped and thought to be reconstituting. But when Charles the Great was crowned emperor in the basilica of St Peter's at Rome by Pope Leo

III on Christmas Day, 800, to many contemporaries it must have seemed a symbol of recovery, a sign that the barbarian was tamed, that Rome had survived and triumphed in the West at Rome as in the East at Constantinople. Charles, king of the Franks and of the Lombards, greatest of the Germanic warchiefs, had re-established the *imperium christianum* of Constantine. The warriors of the Christian king of the Franks, now hailed as emperor, protected the Danube frontier. The Rhine was no longer a frontier. Frankish soldiers, Christian missionaries (especially Anglo-Saxons) and papal emissaries brought faith and sometimes peace to the continental German lands as far as the Elbe and the Harz mountains in the east, and to the borders of Denmark in the north. An amalgam of German and Roman had been triumphantly achieved in the name of Christ. North Africa, Egypt, and the greater part of Spain, and Jerusalem and Syria were, it is true, in Mohammedan hands, but there were signs that the centre of power in the Moslem world was moving east. It was from Baghdad and not from Damascus that the Caliph Haroun-al-Raschid conducted his correspondence and despatched his embassies to the Frankish Charles. At Constantinople, Irene, the empress of the second Rome, watched uneasily the progress of the Franks in the West. The Eastern Empire, as it now may be called, possessed political control of Asia Minor, and by constant labour retained its foothold in the south of Italy, Sicily, and the islands of the Eastern Mediterranean. Its strength, and increasingly its reason of being, lay in Constantinople, Miklegarth, the great city, as the Vikings were to come to term it, the pivot of world trade between west and east. Now in the face of the two world blocks that had emerged from the ruins of Rome, Byzantium and the Moslem Empire, the West also had precariously achieved its unity, a new unity it might be said, with a literal reorientation. The continental Germans, Saxons, Thuringians, Bavarians, Suabians, and Franconians had been brought within the pale of Romanic, Christian civilization. A third world force had been created. Frankish counts and Christian bishops, *comites episcopique*, were brought to the fringe of territories inhabited by hostile Slavs and powerful Northerners. Byzantium would penetrate culturally much though not all of the Slav territory. Western concerns now lay increasingly with the West Slavs, Wends, Poles, Czechs, Slovaks, and – the central point in our story – with the Scandinavians.

Such broad and sweeping generalizations have their moments of truth and also their dangers. From the ethnic point of view it is only too easy to see the period 400–800 as the time when the German peoples, including the Anglo-Saxons, were converted to a Roman-based civilized way of life with the Christian church, the heir of Rome, acting as the principal agent. Our Viking Age then is the next stage forward. By 1100 the Christian religion was accepted in Greenland, in Iceland, and throughout the Scandinavian world. Christian dynasties that looked to Rome were dominant among the Poles, the Czechs, and even the non-Slavonic Hungarians. The centralized and centralizing papacy of Hildebrand, Pope Gregory VII 1073–85, influenced a wider territory than that embraced in the western part of the territorial state of Rome. Who were these Northerners, the Scandinavians, so painfully brought into the orbit of Christendom? What standard of civilization had they reached at the time of the coronation of Charles the Great? Why were they about to constitute at that stage in European development a new and fearful threat to the Western world? These are the questions which have provoked so much recent thought and writing on the Northern world.

Scandinavia towards the end of the eighth century

We rely principally on archæological and linguistic evidence for our picture of Scandinavia in the pre-Viking period. The dominant elements in the population were Germanic, pagan and substantially illiterate, though the continuous and sustained use of runes indicates moves in the direction of literacy and therefore of a more settled order. Folk movements in the fifth century, including a substantial emigration of Angles west into Frisia and England, had resulted in a degree of underpopulation. Yet the sixth and seventh centuries represent a quiet period politically with some evidence of prosperity. Rich grave finds from the Vendel period in Sweden suggest trading contacts with the Frankish and Mediterranean world, and proof of wealth among the ruling princes. Danish archaeologists are also uncovering evidence that southern Scandinavia was enjoying relative prosperity in the immediate pre-Viking Age. A climatic amelioration appears to have helped the Scandinavians to achieve stability and so to establish a powerful base in men and materials for their enterprises. Religiously there appears to have been a basic uniformity of belief. The Scandinavians followed common Germanic custom in burial ceremonies and fertility rites. Their gods were the familiar Germanic gods, Tiw, Odin (Woden), Thor and Frey (Freyja). A special twist, however, was given both to belief and to ceremonies because of the harsh economic and climatic conditions of much of the North. The hard necessity of reliance on self and companions in the bitter struggle against the climate and natural conditions led to a curious attitude of equality towards the gods. The Scandinavian did not creep to the altar. The gods themselves were subject to testing and open to rejection if a stronger deity than they appeared. There are accounts of formal sacrificial ceremonies. Ship-burial (the ultimate product of northern thought concerning ritual) represented one of the most elaborate methods known to mankind for the disposal of the body of the dead. Everyday routine and seasonal change were accompanied by religious ceremonial. Each head of household possessed sacrificial rights, and the kings, when they appeared, enjoyed a sacral quality. A specialist priesthood did not develop. There is little trace of a class of men set apart from other men by their professional career of worship of the gods. In the hard world of the North, such a luxury could not be afforded: men were needed at battle, plough, and bed.

The Scandinavians were polytheistic. A multiplicity of gods governed the cycle of the years. Some strong elements of nature worship persisted and were further to persist until and beyond the end of heathendom. Fountains, streams and groves were regarded as specially sacred. Cults were built around veneration for the oak or the ash. The heavens in their mysteries, sun, moon, thunder and lightning, attracted the worshipper. In more sophisticated form regeneration themes can faintly be traced in the attitudes to the rising sun on the cycle of human growth from conception to death and decay. By the opening of the Viking Age three cults were clearly coming to predominate within the Northern pantheon: the worship of Odin (Woden), Thor and Frey. Under stress of the Viking Age and ceaseless activity Thor came to predominate, notably in Iceland, though Odin continued to draw much support, notably from the articulate poets and nobles who cared for wisdom, even for the wisdom of the serpent, more than for strength. In essence Thor was a sky-god, Jove the Thunderer. His symbols were the hammer, the axe, and probably the swastika. Physical strength was his prime attribute. He regulated the weather. Seafarers turned to him in their peril. Odin developed into a much more sophisticated being. In the North he became the god of cunning in the true sense of the word, knowledge as well as craft. He was the god who would beguile the wayfarer, the one-eyed to be encountered at cross-roads, the wily protector. Frey was the fertility god, hermaphroditic in most elaborate form, protector of crops, of sex and the harvest. There is some evidence that his cult was more fully developed in Sweden than any of the other Scandinavian communities.

Other gods and supernatural beings also abounded and are among the best known figures of Scandinavian thought to the modern world. Balder, the beautiful and Loki, the evil genius of the gods, are known as well as, if not better than, the figures of Greek mythology. But they in final form are the product of the high imagination of a sophisticated literary civilization of the twelfth and thirteenth centuries. They represent the triumph of antiquarian reconstruction. As such, our Tales from Asgarth tell us much of the fine achievements of Icelandic civilization; they only reflect dimly, and sometimes distort grossly, the gods of the Viking Age.

The same must be said of the fundamental tenets of belief of the Scandinavian. In finished literary form, as seen through the writings of Snorri Sturluson, the Scandinavians had a most elaborate mythology. Man's struggle in this world was an incident, an episode, on his way to the next. Essentially it was a testing-time. If the test were successfully taken, the warrior would, after death in battle, weapon in hand, enter Valhalla where a place would be prepared for him. The choosers of the slain would proffer him wine. He would live the life of a chosen companion until the gods would lead him out on the last fight against the snake that encompassed the earth, against the powers of evil. The fight would end in disaster. The Twilight of the Gods would end in deep night. Things won – or lost – were done; all joy lay in the doing. Such myth was the product of long centuries, much influenced by parallel Christian beliefs. Echoes of it can, however, be traced back to the earliest poetry. The boldness and in a sense the completeness of the fully formulated pattern should not blind us to the essential inadequacy and immaturity of the religion for a settled civilization and people. Perpetuation of the life of the military camp is a poor ideal to set against the subtler spiritual force of Christianity.

Nevertheless, similarity of belief, even if sometimes tenuously held, served as a unifying force among the Scandinavians. More important perhaps is a cognate similarity in language and institutions.

Our knowledge of the spoken tongue of the Viking Age is necessarily patchy, the evidence surviving from runic inscriptions, many on memorial stones, and from fossilized forms in place-names and proper names. Primitive Norse was differentiated from continental German slowly during the period c.AD 100–700, and this differentiation was accelerated during the Viking Age, though with close affinities retained with the Western Germanic languages. Inside the Northern world some clear-cut distinctions took place from about AD 1000, and probably earlier if the evidence derived from British place-names can fully be taken into account. The changes were exact enough to enable us to separate Old West Norse from Old East Norse, the parent tongues of modern Norwegian and Icelandic on the one hand and of modern Swedish and Danish on the other; but such changes were slight within the structure of the language as a whole. For practical purposes only one tongue was spoken in the North during the Viking Age.

Institutional life also exhibited features common to the whole of Scandinavia with only minor regional variants. Kingship had developed and was still developing within all the communities, not extensive territorial kingship, but the recognized existence of certain kindreds which because of their pre-eminence in war were known as royal. These kindreds enjoyed special legal privileges, and special rights and duties, in large part religious as well as military, were also associated with them. In southern Norway one dynasty, the Ynglings, had risen to special prominence and dominated the lands around the Oslo fjord. A cognate dynasty had reached the height of political achievement in the prehistoric period in Sweden, and the great grave mounts of Old Uppsala and the Vendel period still testify to its magnificence. We also know of many other dynasties, among the Geats in what is now southern Sweden but was then an integral part of the Danish world, among the Danes themselves at Leire in Zealand, and at Jelling in Jutland, around Bergen in the western fjords of Norway and far to the north among the men of Trondheim. The title of king was much less exclusive than among some of the German peoples of the Western folk-wandering. It was used freely by many male adults of a royal kin. Institutions associated with kingship were weak. The kings lacked the apparatus of dependent local government, and of the tenacious and sometimes blind support of a literate clerisy, without which permanent active life was difficult in these centuries. They were essentially warlords whose wealth and power were sometimes glorious, but often brief and precarious.

There also existed a class of earls or jarls sometimes difficult to distinguish from the king but clearly lacking both the pagan sanctions and the special dignity which went with the royal kindreds. These seem to have been prominent in the Norwegian lands, notably in the fjords of the south west and west where the sheer isolation of geography may well have led to the emergence of a number of powerful families, no one able to sustain supremacy but all gaining enough from their lordship over several small fjord settlements to raise their families above the commonalty. They also had come by the opening of the Viking Age to enjoy special legal privileges in return presumably for the protection they were able to offer the folk.

The basic unit in society, however, was no king or earl but a *bondi*, a free farmer, roughly equivalent to the Anglo-Saxon ceorl. It is well from the outset to disabuse ourselves of misleading democratic notions. The *bondi* was no little man in our sense of the word. He was at his most typical the head of a household, a man of some property in land and especially in stock. He was a slave-owner. His symbols of rank were his axe and his spear. The mark of the freeman was the right to bear arms. He was oath-worthy and law-worthy with a right to assist at the making of judgements at the local court. Sturdy, and at times savage, independence was a characteristic of this breed, but we must remember how his very litigious and squabblesome nature found its outlet in what was essentially communal institutional life, in the folk-court, the local *thing*, held at some traditional spot in forest, heath or grove, marked by some memorial of stone or wood, hallowed by long custom already by the end of the eighth century.

There was, therefore, a certain unity in social structure characteristic of the whole of the Scandinavian lands at the beginning of the Viking Age. Some of the features were, it is true, common to all the Germanic world, but the economic backwardness and the localism bred of such poverty exaggerated Scandinavian peculiarities: the petty king and earl, the *bondi* and the unfree thrall were the typical units in this Northern society. Only in some favoured areas were these signs of a stirring towards greater things, towards a kingship that would extend over a wider area. The Viking Age can never be seen in proper perspective unless it is realised that the terrifying raids overseas were co-terminous with the first stirrings towards national unity within Scandinavia itself. We have to this point stressed Scandinavian uniformity. Differences also existed, differences natural to communities which dwelt in habitats as varied as the rugged fjords of the Sogn and Hardanger, the fertile low-lands of Leire or Ribe, or the savage lands of Halogaland (modern Nordland), further north than other men dwelt. By 1100 these differences had been given political shape and permanent form by the creation of three kingdoms of Norway, Sweden and Denmark. In 800 the shape could be discerned, but the permanence was far from certain.

Three dynasties, in fact, began to emerge from the complexities of the social situation. All three owed much to favourable conditions in land, in stock, and above all in control of communications. Most prominent among the dynasties in 800 was the Danish house of Leire near Roskilde in Zealand. Carolingian pressure against Saxons and Frisians had brought Christendom to its doorstep. King Godfred (*c.*800–810) provided a weighty answer to Frankish pride, and Danish pirates gave trouble to the emperor Charles the Great himself in his last years when border wars threatened the precarious Carolingian peace. An uneasy truce which laid the pattern of future development was established by the death of Charles the Great: on the Frankish side of the border special Marcher lordships were set up; on the Danish side great physical barriers in the form of defensive earthworks were built or extended. Godfred was responsible for developing the *Danevirke*, the first important stage of which appears to have been built as early as *c.*AD 737, a massive system ultimately aimed at protecting the whole Jutland peninsula from the Slie fjord to the North Sea. Godfred's primary concern was probably to protect Hedeby against the Franks and their now dependent Saxons. His dynasty survived with mixed fortunes. Attempts on the part of the missionary Anskar to convert the Danes from his two centres of Hamburg and Bremen were not successful, though Christian churches were set up, presumably for the use of Christian merchants, at Hedeby and Ribe – and at Birka in Sweden. Sporadic raiding south continued throughout the ninth century, and Hamburg itself was sacked in 845. Little can be deduced about the internal authority of the Danish kings. Two of them, Sigfred and Godfred, were killed in a disastrous campaign on the Dyle in 891, a victory which pointed the way to final recovery on the part of the East Frankish or German realm. Ohthere (a Norwegian sea-captain) and Wulfstan (probably an Englishman), who gave King Alfred a graphic account of their voyages to the North and into the Baltic, are clear enough, however, about the continued integrity of the idea of Denmark as a geographical unit which included Jutland and the islands and Danish territories in what is now Sweden (i.e. Skåne), though not Bornholm, which had its own king, nor Blekinge, which was Swedish. But the end of the ninth century and the beginning of the tenth proved a period of political confusion which culminated in the submission of a large part of Denmark to the rule of Swedish kings.

In 800 the glory of the Swedish dynasty, the Ynglings, lay in the past. Rich treasures from the Dark Ages have been found in the grave-mounds of old Uppsala. The kings who gave their name to the period, and the craftsmen who contributed the first Vendel goods flourished mightily in the sixth and seventh centuries AD. The exploits of some of these kings of the Suear in the east-central plains of Sweden are hinted at in the English epic *Beowulf*. Many believe that the Swedes may have influenced directly the English dynasty of East Anglia. There was a period in the seventh and eighth centuries when the vigour of the dynasty expressed itself in external expansion. The big island of Öland lay under Swedish control. Gotland became an important Swedish centre. Clear evidence of early Viking settlement appears in Grabin in the Baltic lands. But the Swedish dynasty was in something of a backwater at the time the Viking Age opened, and it was not until the late ninth century or the initial decades of the tenth that Swedish kings emerged as an important force in internal Scandinavian politics when for a long generation (prompted probably by commercial motives) Swedish rulers governed the by now key settlement at Hedeby and a good portion of South Jutland.

Norway was as backward politically as Sweden in the early ninth century. The Westfold dynasty of the Ynglings, centred around the district of modern Tonsberg, had emerged as the most powerful group, the men of the Vik, but their power had waned. It was not until the later years of the century, a generation after the first onslaught of Viking hordes, that the dynasty re-emerged triumphant. Their triumph is associated with the greatest name in early Norwegian history, that of Harold Fairhair. It is hard to disentangle the facts of his reign from the legendary accretions that have gathered around his name, but some things are clear. He was of the true Ynglings line of the Westfold princes, the son of Halfdan the Black. He succeeded his father at an early age, probably in the 870s when he was still only ten. He had a very long reign which straddled the most creative generations of Viking political advance, died at an uncertain date though later than 931, and was buried not in his native lands of the Oslo fjord but in Rogaland in south-west Norway.

During his lifetime he established the idea if not always the practice of a unified Norwegian kingship. The men of the North, the Trondelag, recognized his overlordship. His massive contribution was made in the West, the focal point for so much of the Viking enterprise west over sea. Quite early in his reign, almost certainly between 885 and the end of the century, Harold won a sea victory at Hafrsfjord, not far from Stavanger, against a strong federacy of petty kinglets and jarls of the west and south west. The victory was decisive in Harold's personal career and to some extent in Norway's history. Harold took to the south west and the west (Hardanger, the orchard of Norway). He made it his favoured home, protected it from incursions back from dissident Vikings settled overseas, used it as his base for fierce punitive expeditions to the Scottish Isles, perhaps even to Ireland, and finally was buried there instead of in his ancestral home on the Oslo fjord. The men of the West were long to maintain their sturdy independence. But Harold deserves the traditional political credit ascribed to him for bringing the lands of the western fjords into close relationship with the lands and dynasty of the Vik.

It used to be the custom (particularly when the date of 872 was ascribed to the battle) to interpret Harold Fairhair's victory of Hafrsfjord as the true beginning of the full Viking Age. Many, including contemporaries, attributed the main force of the Viking onslaught, particularly the onslaught on England, to the dissatisfaction caused to active, turbulent young Scandinavian jarls and sea-captains by the discipline imposed by new and more effective kings. This view is no longer held. It was always difficult to reconcile with the known facts of the Danish situation, and even in a Norwegian context made only partial sense. It is more important to recognize Hafrsfjord as a step in the making of Norway, and to remember that the Viking outburst and the consolidation of the communities into larger kingdoms at home were contemporary and related processes.

If dissatisfaction and consolidation at home cannot be given pride of place among the reasons for the Viking outbursts, what other possibilities exist? Climatic reasons may be identified, but they are certainly not simple. On the whole, the Viking Age was a warm and dry period in the history of the north and west of Europe, leading to a climatic optimum in the central Middle Ages, *c.*1050–1250. Only for the two or three generations, *c.*860–940, is there evidence for temporarily colder conditions in Scandinavia, a vital period it is true for migration and settlement in Britain and in Normandy. Later in the Middle Ages the climate worsened dramatically with a peak of severity *c.*1430 and disastrous consequences on Nordic settlement in Greenland and on the prosperity of Iceland. But as far as origins are concerned, progressive gelidation cannot be held to account for the Viking outburst of the ninth century.

Pressure of population on resources is a different matter. Population losses suffered in the fifth century AD appear to have been made good by the end of the ninth century, and much earlier in some regions. There was some immigration, or reverse migration, more perhaps than used to be allowed, and the Heruli and Burgundians have left faint traces of such movement north. Most important, however, was natural increase as communities tightened their control of initially isolated settlements and achieved a better mastery of farming conditions and ploughing techniques under an improving climate. Yet, to judge from the historical record, such population increase did not apply uniformly. Denmark, potentially the most fruitful and fertile part of Scandinavia, was something of laggard. Sweden enjoyed only a partial intensification of rural activity and rural population, enough, to be sure, to establish permanent and advance posts in the eastern Baltic in the seventh century. Norway provides the best evidence. For at some time in the eighth century there began a small but steady colonizing movement from the western fjords of Norway to the islands to the north and north west of the Scottish mainland.

Dating the movement to the Northern Isles is not easy because it was continuous until at least the end of the tenth century. In the Orkneys Norwegian settlers appear to have encountered a weak Pictish settlement, and by *c.*AD 800, established a social dominance which converted the islands into virtually a pure form of Norse society: attempts to plant themselves on the mainland were less successful with only a few isolated settlements in Caithness and Ross at this stage. In the Shetlands evidence for Celtic settlement in depth is weak, and it is likely that the Vikings found large tracts of potentially useful land unoccupied. Further to the north in the Faroes, initially in the early ninth century and in greater intensity in the latter half of the century the Norwegians settled land inhabited by only a few Celtic hermits. Iceland, the king-pin in Norwegian colonizing history, was heavily and systematically settled, *c.*870–930, with the help of significant elements, largely servile, from the Celtic world. To the west in the Hebrides settlement was carried out with greater political difficulty and a much more balanced mixture of peoples, Celtic and Norse. More will be said later of all these matters. For the moment it is well to reflect on them as our best indication of some overpopulation and urge to find new lands in at least one part of the Scandinavian world. The need must have been great to compel men and women and their families to attempt settlement on the bleak, windswept, and often barren, islands of the North Atlantic.

The success of these early colonizing moves gives proof of two other powerful elements in the story of early Viking expansion: Scandinavian skill at boat-construction and Scandinavian skill at stock-breeding, notably the care and maintenance of sheep. The Viking longship captures admiration by its sheer beauty. It is the end product of a long line of trial and error in northern waters, leading from the crudity of the ships which brought the Anglo-Saxon migrants to Britain, through the evolution of the sailing ships with true keel to the final flexible beauty of Gokstad, as fine a creation as could be achieved, given the limitations of tools and materials available in the period. The less spectacular transport and trading vessels of the period, too, the knörrs, as they are commonly termed, were fine technical achievements. To arrive and to raid was one thing; to settle quite another. It is here that Norse and Celtic skill at animal husbandry must have come into its own. Such skills leave little trace; but without them the Scandinavian long, cautious, and highly successful occupation of the Northern Isles of Britain, the Faroes and of Iceland itself, would have been impossible.

Much more trace, of course, has remained of the shipbuilding skill, and it is interesting to see how modern scholars turn to it time and time again in their search for reasons for the Viking outbursts. The very nature of most of Scandinavia made the need for good water communications obvious. In the western fjords, for example, where communication to this day is mostly by water, communities could not exist in number until they had mastered the art of steady and reliable transport along the waterways. An odd feature of physical geography specially favoured the dweller in western Norway. The coastline itself along the whole massive length of the Norwegian seaboard is protected from the worst of the Atlantic gales by a series of islands which help to break to some extent the force of wind and tide. The great length of many of the fjords also helps to give protection and to calm the waters. The inner recesses of the Sogn and the Hardanger, to take two obvious examples, provide as splendid a training ground for builders and users of deep-water craft as can be found anywhere in the world. Time and some generations of peace were needed, but the skills once obtained were not lost until the need for them in turn disappeared in the modern world. Timber was in plentiful supply. The same ships which took peaceful colonizers to the Faroes could also carry young Viking thugs to attack monasteries and farms in peaceful Ireland and Northumbria. Much work has been done recently on the detail of the technical achievements. The decisive moment of change came somewhere in the late eighth century. Ships earlier than that date, the Kvalsund ship, for example, were still predominantly rowing boats, capable of adaptation for sailing, but probably still of doubtful stability and incapable of continuous sailing for long stretches in Atlantic water. The maturing of the techniques of building ships with a heavy true keel and the development of methods of measuring the strakes more accurately and of keying in hull and ribs and deck more precisely ensured greater stability and flexibility. The late eighth and early ninth centuries was the period during which the art of the Scandinavian boat-builder was brought to a high point of perfection, and it no coincidence that Viking activity originated during the same period. Trustworthy, easily manoeuvrable vessels, fast-moving and of shallow draught were an essential and basic element in Viking movement and achievement.

Our best evidence comes from archaeological sources of a dramatic kind, from the Viking ships miraculously preserved in the blue clay of the Oslo fjord, at Oseberg and particularly at Gokstad, and from the more recent finds made of sunken blockships (of the central Viking period) at Skuldelev in the Roskilde fjord. For earlier Viking technical achievement the evidence of the Gokstad ship stands supreme. In 1880 archaeologists discovered at Gokstad on the west side of the Oslo fjord, some fifty miles from Oslo itself, under a funerary mound, a fine ship, with fittings and grave goods, in an astonishing state of preservation. It was a sailing ship, nearly 80 feet long, $17\frac{1}{2}$ feet in breadth at its widest point, and some 6 feet, 5 inches from keel to gunwale at its maximum height. It was built substantially of oak, with only the decking, the mast, the yards and the oars of pine. The keel consisted of a single timber nearly 60 feet long, so substantial in fact that when a replica was built in 1892 the designers had to use Canadian oak for want of suitable straight solid oak timber in Scandinavia itself. The planking consisted of 16 strakes of varying thickness, most of them 1 inch thick but with extra breadth coming at the water-line (the tenth strake of $1\frac{3}{4}$ inches) and at the line of the oar-holes (the fourteenth strake of $1\frac{1}{4}$ inches). The fifteenth and sixteenth strakes were very thin (only $\frac{7}{12}$ inches) and were capped by a heavy gunwale of $4\frac{1}{4}$ inches by $3\frac{1}{12}$ inches. The hull was clinker built, and the ingenuity of the construction, notably the variation of thickness of the strakes, the spacing of the ribs and the keying-in of deck to hull, permitted maximum flexibility. The side-rudder, which extended 18 inches below the keel, permitted easy handling even in rough waters. The overall weight was $8\frac{1}{2}$ tons, or 10 tons fully laden. Oars were available for movement in shallow waters or in emergency. The replica built in 1892 crossed the Atlantic in less than a month in April 1893. Captain Magnus Andersen, who was in command, praised the ship for the elasticity and flexibility in handling which enabled it to reach speeds of over 10 knots in relative comfort in spite of an unsophisticated rigging. The Gokstad ship was the product of perhaps a century or a century and a half of experiment that finally enabled the Norsemen to command the northern seas. By 800 the technical knowledge needed to construct the longships and the more prosaic maid-of-all-work transports and traders had been acquired. All that was needed were men with the will and resources to direct their energies to making use of these magnificent instruments of movement, trade, and war.

It would be wrong, however, to lay so much emphasis on the material achievement, the ships, to the neglect of the men who made them and the men who used them. Two further aspects of the Northerners' attainments and attitudes seem directly relevant to their activities in the late eighth and early ninth centuries. Skill in constructing ships is quite different from skill in navigation. How did the Scandinavians, and one thinks especially of the Norwegians in this respect, make the leap forward to face navigation across the open seas of the Atlantic and the North Sea? Later sagas tell of the existence of a sun-stone, a rudimentary compass, though information about such an instrument is vague and dubious. Long experience and detailed knowledge of the stars and of the migration routes of birds are better attested and more relevant to their early success. Detailed tables of the sun's midday latitude week by week throughout the year appear to have been known in tenth-century Iceland. A bearing-dial from twelfth-century Greenland suggests a quite sophisticated division of the navigation circle into sixteen segments. With sufficient grasp of the apparent position of the midday sun (and of the Polar Star) effective mastery of vital information about the ship's latitude could be ensured. Norse sailing directions that survive are for the most part terse assessments of so many days' sailing on a direct reckoning. It would be wrong and misleading to underestimate the weight of navigational aids and experience at the Norseman's disposal, but perhaps even more compelling than the existence of their technical navigational skills were the reasons, psychological and sociological why so many men were willing to invest their resources and to take the formidable risks involved in such journeyings. These were no ill-equipped hordes in fear of imminent starvation. What explanations can be offered of their attitudes? What did they seek from the outer world?

The answers that come most readily to mind are status, and the spoils of war: treasure, material possession and womenfolk. National or religious pride played no great part in the ventures, though there may have been an element of protective reaction against the threat passed by Christian missions to the established social order. The Vikings were no *herrenvolk*; even less so were they missionaries. The recognized political leaders in Scandinavia were not Vikings. Only slowly did raiding and royal prestige become associated. The intense moves of the late ninth century may be read as reaction against the political consolidation attempted by rising kingship; they were certainly not a direct impulse towards consolidation of kingship. The initial Viking raids were joint-stock ventures, private, personal, and matters essentially for the young. Yet the release of so much energy and turbulence overseas gave stay-at-home dynasties a wonderful opportunity. Parallels spring to mind with the Moslem world, though there a religion which prohibited fighting any fellow-believers played an important part. Parallels also exist, in a later more settled period, with the Norman world in the eleventh century when a similar release of turbulent aristocratic energy to Spain, to Italy, to England and on Crusade, helped both Norman dukes and French kings to build up permanent institutions of territorial government.

Status is a difficult sociological concept, easy to recognise, hard to define. Possession of a free kindred, possession of land, and valour in war were the three principal sources of status in early Viking times. In this respect several possibilities emerge as worthy of enquiry in relation to the motives which sent so many young men a-Viking. Overpopulation in the absolute sense may not have been a decisive factor, except in the hard lands of western Norway.

Overpopulation in selected classes of society is a very different matter. When we first glimpse the land-law of the North, we find that odal-right, while making ample provision for the eldest son, contrasts vigorously with a system of primogeniture. Every son had his right in the parental homestead. Survival of even three sons from each family could therefore lead to dislocation and social peril for the family group. What evidence we have suggests that the Vikings were adequately prolific. It is reasonable to suppose that the settled middle rung of free farmer bred more children more successfully than other groups: the Scandinavian social system favoured such groups. It would need only a very few settled generations to bring about a state of affairs where the three status factors mentioned above, freedom, land, and opportunity to show and benefit from valour were gravely disturbed. Young sons, or sons more mobile by temperament would look elsewhere, away from the land, for their status achievements.

There remains the question of bravery, valour in war. The Vikings are known by universal reputation as a turbulent crew, not inhibited in any way from internecine warfare. Universal reputation does not always reflect universal truth, and we must not be too misled by lurid stories from saga and poetry, stories chosen often because of their exceptional nature. The Vikings had their own standards. Again, matters of timing, of pure chronology, become very important. Given two or three generations of prosperous farming a network of kindred relationships would be built up over so wide an area that immediate achievement of military prestige would not easily be acquired. Tests of manly strength would result in bootless crimes or wasteful feuds. Quarrels between the more consolidated groups, the men of the Frostathing and the men of the Gulathing, or between Geats and Swedes offered some scope; but these men were basically of the same tongue and type. War overseas was more adventurous and in the initial stages at least much more profitable. Status, difficult to obtain territorially, could be obtained by war, and especially by war overseas. As the young men discovered that status and profit were multiplied a hundred-fold when they turned their aggressive instincts away from their fellow and relatively impoverished Norsemen to the fat lands and monasteries overseas, so did the feeling of solidarity among the Norsemen increase and intensify. Nothing brings human groups together so closely as a shared successful enterprise. Internecine warfare remained a feature and a disgrace to Norse society. To draw the comparison again with the

Mohammedan world, not even the sternest strictures of a new world religion could keep the Moslem world from savage internal warfare for more than a generation. But the first generation could be vital: the back of the defensive systems protecting the southern arc of the fertile crescent was broken in the first generation after Mahomet's death (632–60) and before civil war racked the new Mohammedan world. On a smaller scale in northern waters the second half of the ninth century represented a corresponding period.

Both status and bravery were naturally closely associated with the spoils of war, sheer loot from piracy. Precious goods, slaves, men and women, all the proceeds of a material civilization greater than their own, acted as a bait and as a spur for Viking ventures. Yet even this simple proposition is not as simple as it seems. Loot was and remained an incentive as late as the eleventh century. But it was often associated with other forms of gain which serve as a reminder of the complexity of this phase in human history. The same men could be pirates one day, colonizers the next, and peaceful traders again the third. Instances can be multiplied, even in the high Viking period, of ships' crews setting off jauntily, uncertain whether to trade or loot. Many of the most successful chieftains and sea-captains were opportunists of the first order, as ready to turn an honest as a dishonest penny, if the opposition to piracy looked too dangerous. Coolness of judgement and an ability to gauge the odds was as characteristic of the successful Viking chief as his legendary bravery and audacity. Nor must we forget that the colonization enterprises, rightly praised, in the northern islands and indeed over large sections of Britain and part of Normandy, were not matters for small family units of freemen working in isolation. In the North land was won by hard toil against savage climatic conditions. Slave labour was a much to be desired asset. Our best information comes from Iceland and there, as we know, from the great record of the land-taking which has remained from the period 870–930, Celtic thralls were a feature of this earliest stage in settlement. Indeed some of the credit which, as has been mentioned earlier, goes rightly to the Norseman for animal husbandry should in equity be shared by their Celtic slaves, from time immemorial associated with the shepherd's craft. Social historians stress the importance to the economy of this early period of the intelligent use of summer pasturage at shielings often quite remote from the main farm; the Celtic word -arg (argh) is frequently found in northern place-names (*ærgi*, for example, is Faroese) to describe such shielings. The elegiac lament of the modern Welsh poet may well have sounded over Faroe fell and Icelandic dale.

> O God, why makest thou the Vale of Aurland so beautiful
> And the life of an old shepherd so short?

While Celtic shepherds and Irish princesses are to be found, the ones on the farms and the other in the genealogies of many Icelandic freeholders, the need for servile labour was no less to his kinsman further south, in Ireland, Northumbria, Eastern Mercia or the Cotentin. Here the fight was against man rather than nature. Freedom among the small landowners remained a characteristic of Scandinavianized north-western Europe, but so did thraldom. Even after settlement the incentive for successful slave-raiding was not removed.

More important perhaps than the slaving and sheer garnering of loot was the association with relatively peaceful trading. This aspect of Viking life is only just beginning to receive its proper due in connection with the reason for the outbreak. In Roman times Scandinavia may have been something of a backwater, but not an unknown backwater. In particular, knowledge of the amber-bearing qualities of the Baltic was commonplace to the Romans, and a well-beaten route extended from the Empire through Denmark to the lands known historically as East Prussia and Lithuania. No regular trade route existed in the sixth and seventh centuries: the times were not propitious. But in the eighth there is firm evidence of revived contact. Within Scandinavia itself three areas emerged as settlements through which contact with the Christian world could be effected. In modern-day Sweden the townships of Birka on the great lake Mälar gave their first sign of organized trading life about this period. In Norway the archaeologist has found at Skiringssal (to the south of the western shore of the Oslo fjord) evidence of trading that may well go back to the earliest period. Denmark, of immense importance in this respect in the ninth century, is a more difficult case. Excavations at Ribe have given conclusive proof of trading activity there from the early eighth century. Hedeby, at the head of Slie fjord in modern Schleswig, presents special problems. Some traders may have been active as early as the late eighth century: military and political endeavour are more characteristic of the scanty records which remain. It is no accident that the three trading centres of Birka, Skiringssal and Hedeby, are all associated with areas that later come to be important dynastic headquarters. The joint growth (and mutual advantage gained by proximity) of kingship and honest trade was a matter of prime interest for the future development of western Europe. For our purpose, the isolation of reasons for the Viking outburst, it is sufficient to mention the fact that the revival of regular trade, with all that implies in the way of knowledge of routes and resources appears to have occurred at roughly the same period as the earlier Viking attacks. The tangled web of trade and piracy continued to spread through the Viking period. We remember the Norseman as a founder of fortified markets as well as a despoiler of churches.

Contemporaries, puzzled and fearful, attempted also to isolate the reasons for these savage attacks from the North. Many dismissed them as an act of God. The record-makers were Christian and churchmen, who talked in terms of a heathen scourge. Indeed it is often pointed out that our picture of Vikings are at times highly coloured because so much of their energy was directed against a church they had no reason to respect and whose goods they coveted. No wonder the clerical historians talked of spring fertility rites and polygamy which to their minds led straight to problems of overpopulation. Undoubtedly, too, the speed and mobility of the attacks led to a further strengthening of the view that here was indeed a heathen visitation brought about because of the sins of the people. The Northern capacity for long continuous journeying and for long campaigns remained a mystery to the more settled folk of the West. None of the voyaging, except to Greenland and Vinland and around the North Cape, was completely new to Western experience. It was the knitting together of known short routes into a long continuous and almost routine whole that rightly impressed the Western world. The supernatural element did not together wear off, even after longer acquaintance. Their language was obviously cognate at least to the English and to the continental German. Their religious and some of their social customs were not. They came into Western experience at an odd moment in the life of the Western world. Ideas of a larger unity in the Carolingian world were deeply tinged with religious thought: Christendom not Europe was the general conception behind advanced political thought. Charles the Great had been crowned and the Empire formed that the heathen might not mock the Christian. Not mockery but butchery, robbery, and deep affliction was the fate of much of this new-found Christendom at the hands of these heathen invaders.

To this point we have looked largely at the inner life of the Scandinavian world to find reasons for the Viking outburst. In conclusion it is necessary to look briefly again at the peoples they attacked. Some political cause of their success, as has already been suggested, can be found in the very nature of the formation of the Carolingian Empire. Destruction of Frisian sea-power, in particular, made the way easier for Viking seafarers. More important still is the simple fact of disunity underlying the new imperial fabric. Economic resources would not permit unitary government to be sustained over so large an area. Squabbles, and senseless feuding of successor princes, gave the Scandinavians ever-increasing scope for action. Britain lay on the fringe, open to the North. Some of the same inadequacies that applied to the Carolingian Empire applied also to her political structure. It is with the British polity that our next chapter will be chiefly concerned.

2

Britain at the beginning of the Scandinavian invasions

It has rightly been held that the barbarian invasions of the ninth and early tenth centuries represented an onslaught against Christian Europe. The attackers, notably the Magyars and the Scandinavians, were aggressively non-Christian. Conversion and the slackening of onslaught arrived together. In the North the triumph of cross over hammer marks the end of the Viking Age. In the first instance, however, religion had little to do with the enterprises. Wealth and political weakness were the more obvious spurs to attack: and raids slackened as they grew more dangerous and less profitable. Ultimately the feudal lord and the rudimentary castle checked the barbarian onslaught.

Of all areas of western Europe Britain and Ireland endured most from the northern barbarians. Geographical factors, sheer proximity to sea-raiders capable of taking the North Sea in their stride, accounted for much. There were also deep political and economic reasons why this should be so.

Britain itself was, in AD 800 divided into many political and ethnic groups, each under its own king, Saxon, Briton, Scot or Pict. The common ground was Christianity. At the Synod of Whitby in 663 a decision was taken whereby in matters affecting the dating of Easter, baptism, and the tonsure of monks, Roman practice rather than the indigenous Celtic forms would be observed. Gradually the native Celtic communities followed the Northumbrian example. Rome became dominant in polity as well as custom. Free intercourse was achieved between Celtic and Germanic missionaries. The Celts, and particularly the Irish, became famous throughout Europe, and above all in the well-beaten paths that lay through the monastic houses of St Gall and of Bobbio on the way to Rome. English missionaries concentrated more on the continental German lands. The greatest of their number, Boniface, Winfrith of Crediton in Devon, martyred by the Frisians in 755, is rightly known as the Apostle of the Germans. Britain remained outside the political structure of the Carolingian Empire. Her men, Irish, Saxon, Welsh, and Scottish were deep in the heart of the Christian church, a most active and dynamic element in the ecclesiastical and spiritual life of Western Christendom.

A similar coincidence of aim and achievement among the communities of Britain can be found in the artistic field. The late seventh century had seen the blossoming of a cultural movement into what is often termed the Northumbrian Renaissance. New vitality and intensity of artistic experience was reflected in the supreme products of the age, the Northumbrian gospel-books of which the Lindisfarne Gospels, the Book of Durrow, and the Book of Kells give us our finest extant examples. Stone crosses, sculpture, and skill in church building also indicate the strength of the artistry of the period. Nor were the literary arts neglected. In the person of Bede, theologian, historian, and scientist, Northumbria produced the outstanding scholar of his age. This renaissance was no mere sudden flaring-up of cultural activity with no future to it. The eighth century was a very troubled century politically. Church life was disrupted, and evidence of some corruption and falling-off in standards is easy to find. But the main stream of cultural and literary life remained powerful. Archbishop Egbert's school and library at York were among the best known in Christendom. The outstanding scholar at the court of Charles the Great, Alcuin, later abbot of Tours, had been trained at that school. From the Celtic world Irish scholars continued their fabled peregrination, carrying with them their typical flair for ascetic observance and scholarly extravagance. Hisperic Latin was the badge of their origins, and pride of their schools. Diversity existed in obvious and manifold ways in Britain. It is well to remember the other side of the medal, the common religion, the common observance, the common and joint cultural activity, and the high reputation enjoyed by British scholars and monks throughout Christendom.

In the economic field there was also diversity as well as common experience with a major contrast between the highlands of the north and west and the lowlands of the south and east. The Anglo-Saxons predominated in the drier flatter lands of the south and east: their cereal output was greater. The Celtic peoples dwelt in the more

mountainous and wetter west: the herdsman rather than the ploughman remained the dominant figure in their economy. This simple
distinction, one of emphasis, it must be stressed, had profound
implications for social organization. Cereal-growers had a better
chance of storing a surplus. Stronger royal authority and a stronger
territorial church could and did thrive on such a surplus. Tribal
institutions persist longer in communities where a man's wealth is
reckoned in cattle and sheep. The plough and a money economy
have close and intimate associations.

There is no better indication of economic differences between the
Celtic and Germanic peoples than in their use of coinage. The Celts
struck no coins. The Anglo-Saxons by contrast used coinage freely,
that mark of the ploughman and trader. Even in the seventh century
gold coins were minted at London, and from the later years of that
century through to the end of the eighth a silver coinage of increasingly fine quality was struck by silversmiths working under royal
authority. Within a very few years of the first Viking attacks
on England, in the reign of Offa, king of the Mercians (757–96),
coinage reform brought into being exquisite coins, silver pennies,
that were to remain with only relatively minor modification the
standard current coin of the realm for the succeeding five hundred
years. The penny was struck in the royal name, *Offa rex*. The
existence of a sound silver currency was an economic fact of the first
importance, a clue to the potential wealth of the Anglo-Saxon lands,
and a pointer to the contrast to the coinless Celtic communities of
the period.

The peoples of Britain and Ireland were in an uneasy state of
development in AD 800 with their division into four nations still
not inevitable but clearly foreshadowed. England with its greater
economic resources had progressed further along the path to political unity and strong kingship. The leading dynasty was that of
Mercia, thanks to the reign of King Offa (757–96) who had made
himself effective head of all the Germanic people south of the
Humber. He was a builder of institutions and defender of the church
as well as a military chieftain, and his court was regularly attended
by clerics from all over England. His greatest monument was the
dyke which still bears his name, a massive earthwork that marked
a substantial boundary between the Welsh and the English. His
coinage, his styles, *rex Anglorum*, his courts and his charters show
him as one who made positive contribution to the future unity of
England. With hindsight it is easy to see the weakness of the Mercian

polity, its excessive use of force, its lack of control north of the Humber, the alienation of subordinate peoples, notably in East Anglia and Kent. Wessex proved restive, and in the ninth century under Egbert and his successors proved better able to take the lead in English affairs, decisively during the reign of Egbert's grandson, Alfred the Great (871–99). But by that time the themes of unity and Scandinavian invasion were inextricably tangled.

Political weakness north of the Humber persisted and made a significant contribution to Viking success. In the second half of the seventh century Northumbria had appeared the most powerful kingdom in England. Defeat at the hands of the Picts in 685, civil wars, and the rise of Mercia brought deep disruption, though the church continued to flourish at York, at Jarrow and Wearmouth, and at Lindisfarne. The combination of still wealthy monasteries and ineffective kingship created an irresistible stamping ground for Norse raiders whose most notorious early blows came to fall on Lindisfarne.

Northumbrian turbulence also had its effects to the north. Scotland, as we know it, did not exist, though by 800 there were already identifiable settlement and linguistic patterns that were to emerge full-blown in the medieval kingdom. To begin with, there was a strong Anglo-Saxon element in the south east, northern Bernicia, the Northumbrians dwelling to the north of the Cheviots up to Edinburgh. Political pressure drew them into the orbit of the northern kings, seeking protection from Dunbarton or Stirling rather than Bamborough or York. This territory of Lothian was legally conceded by the powerful English King Edgar in the early 970s to the Scottish king, Kenneth II, in return for an acknowledgement of Edgar's ultimate overlordship. The concession was confirmed after the defeat of an English army at Carham in 1018, an event which rounded off the structure of medieval mainland Scotland.

Concentration on Northumbria and Lothian runs ahead of the main story. We have to look back to the Celtic world to see how Scotland was shaping. The people who were to give their name to the kingdom, the Scots themselves, were only one among the three principal groups of Celtic inhabitants of northern Britain. Their origins lay across the Irish Sea in Ireland. In the difficult days of the fourth and fifth centuries they crossed to the islands and then to the mainland north of the Clyde. Winning an unenviable reputation for themselves for ferocity and piracy they established their kingdom in modern Argyll, in the province which Bede knew as Dalriada (an echo in name of the province of Dalriada in Northern Ireland). They had never been subject to Rome. Their speech was Celtic, Q-Celtic or Goidelic Celtic: that is to say the branch of the Celtic tongue which retained (to mention a conspicuous characteristic) the sound -k- initially in words like *Can* (head) or *cadair* (four) where the other main branches modified the sound to -p- (*Pen*, *pedwar*, in modern Welsh). By c.800 the Scots had effective control of most of the lands from the Great Glen to the isles of Jura, Islay and the peninsula of Kintyre, from the kingdom of Fife to Glasgow. They had been Christianized in the fifth and sixth centuries: St Kentigern and St Columba were their great religious figures. The holy island of Iona was their principal religious centre. Their language was to dominate most of the north and the west of historic Scotland.

Closely associated with them throughout the whole of the period were the most mysterious of all the peoples of these islands, the Picts. It is not even certain that they were Celtic people, though general opinion, acting on the pitifully few scraps of information that can be gleaned from fossilized place-name forms, from the material remains, from the picture-stones of Pictland, and from outside references, now favours strongly Celtic origins for at least the ruling groups among the Picts. The dominant language was a Brythonic dialect, possibly with closer affinities to Gaulish Celtic than to Cumbrian or Welsh. The possibility of the late survival of an indigenous Bronze Age non-Indo-European speaking element among the historic Picts is perhaps the most compelling of the various hypotheses that have been advanced to explain the peculiarities of these people, uncommunicative and yet fertile in artistry. The name Picts, the painted men, was given to them by the Romans, applied to all those who dwelt to the north of the narrow neck of Scotland from the estuary of the Clyde to the Firth of Forth. Christianity reached them from the ministries of St Ninian in the late Roman period, but the results of this British mission were not as deep and permanent as used to be thought. The task of permanent conversion to Christianity took place under the direction of Irish missions led by St Columba. Politically the Picts had been subject to heavy pressure from the British peoples of Strathclyde. The arrival of immigrant Scots into Argyll, with whom they were initially at least often in alliance, further restricted their activities. Northumbrian expansion to the north in the seventh century

(Edinburgh was in English hands from 638) was checked after the Pictish victory at Nechtansmere in 685. Roman Christian observances were adopted by the Picts in the second decade of the eighth century. By 800 they were, however, essentially men of the north east. They had their own customs, including a system of succession to the kingdom through females which later passed for several centuries into Scottish practice. In 843 under the Scottish king, Kenneth MacAlpin, Picts and Scots were brought together in what was to prove an enduring political union. The new Scottish/Pictish kingdom was sometimes known as Scotland but more often, from its ancient Roman designation, as Albany.

The third and last of the Celtic groups of Scotland is different again from the other two. In the south west of the kingdom the political position was confused in the centuries which followed the collapse of Roman military power in Britain. A mixed but predominantly Romano-British population straddled the Wall, and achieved some sort of political shape from the effects of a succession of federate chiefs. These peoples, living in the modern shires of North Lancashire, Westmorland, Cumberland, Dumfries and Ayrshire, extended over an area known by the two territorial designations of Cumbria and Strathclyde. Under Northumbrian pressure in the seventh century most of Cumbria passed under Anglo-Saxon domination, though retaining its essentially Celtic population and at times turning for political leadership to the north, to Traprain Law and *Alclut*. Scandinavian pressure in raids and in settlement had a tremendous impact on the southern (English) part of this area. In 945 Edmund of England ceded all of Cumbria to King Malcolm I of Albany, a great-grandson of Kenneth MacAlpin, in return for a promise of support by sea and by land. It is unlikely that this cession involved territory to the south of the Wall but was meant to apply to Strathclyde. Within the following three-quarters of a century the hold of the Scottish king was strengthened in Strathclyde and with the further gains made in Lothian the shape of the mainland Kingdom of Scotland became fully visible.

There remain the islands but their story is so complicated and so intimately enmeshed with our Scandinavian ventures that it is best treated in detail in an account of the invasions themselves. It is sufficient in this context to note that a whole range of islands, Shetlands, Fair Isle, Orkney, and some of the mainland in the modern shires of Caithness, Ross, Cromarty, and Sutherland, fell under Scandinavian control and were colonized mostly by men of Norwegian

origin. Further west in the Hebrides, and in a range of island settlements again as far south as the Isle of Man, the Vikings settled in
large numbers and came in some areas to predominate in institution
and in language: in other areas, some of which are Gaelic speaking
to this day, they became no more than a formidable minority group.
Their settlements, particularly those in Orkney and the Isle of Man,
constituted strategic centres of the greatest importance, bases and
recruiting grounds for sea-raiders whose mobility by sea was their
greatest single asset.

Mention of the Isle of Man, that stepping-stone in the middle of
the Irish Sea, leads naturally to discussion of the last of the big
political units of the Celtic World, to Wales and to Ireland itself.
Behind Offa's dyke in Wales political groups were also sorting
themselves out into familiar historical shapes. In the latter half of
the seventh and eighth centuries there were, it is true, no kings
or princes of the status of Maelgwn Gwynedd, Cadwallon or
Cadwaladr in earlier generations. The church retained its importance but not as a Romanic unifying force in any way. The political
successes of the age seem to have been made at the local level with
the establishment of more or less permanent divisions of spheres of
influence, the cantrefs of historic Wales. The four principal units
of varying importance and integrity remained the kingdoms of
Deheubarth (from modern Pembroke to Brecon) and Morgannwg
in the south, of Powys (overshadowed by Mercian military might)
in the north east, and Gwynedd in the north west. Only in Gwynedd
in the early ninth century are there signs of promise of larger scale
and more permanent royal institutions. Under Merfyn Frych (the
Freckled) 825–44, something of a cosmopolitan culture developed,
fed no doubt by the wealth of the granaries of Anglesey. In the
event, as we shall see, the strength of his new dynasty coupled with
the toughness of local institutional life was to serve Wales well
during the period of Viking irruption.

Ireland at the end of the eighth century was in a precarious
political state. Its isolation and the migrations to Scotland had left
it in a somewhat underpopulated condition. Agriculture was at a
more backward level than elsewhere in the British Isles, and it was
only as stockraisers that the Irish had a good reputation. Their
equable and damp climate was then, as later, their greatest economic
asset, ensuring as it did an abundance of good pasture. One feature
of Irish life stood as altogether conspicuous and noteworthy in its
age: the religious. Nowhere had Christian missionaries been so

successful as in Ireland. During the Roman occupation of Britain Ireland had been outside the pale and it was not until the decline of the Roman Empire that Christianity reached the Irish shores. The mission of St Patrick in the early fifth century was reinforced in the succeeding two centuries by the very turbulence of this age of migration. Christianity early received a peculiar ascetic twist in Irish society. The dominant element in the polity became not the ordered territorial diocese subject to a bishop as elsewhere in the Christian Roman world. Ireland knew no *civitates* to secure a basis for such ecclesiastical divisions, and instead the monastery, governed by an abbot who was often a prominent tribal figure, became the typical unit in the Irish church. The Irish monks were not however necessarily bound to the cloister. Very full play was given to the individual. Within the community the ascetic ideal was that of the hermit within his cell. Austerities often matched in their extremes the wildness and extremes of nature in which the early monasteries were planted: the rocky fortresses off the west Irish coast or the windswept banks of the northern lochs. Missionary enterprise was also actively encouraged as one among the austere practices that signalled salvation. In the sixth century Irish enterprise concentrated on the North: their chief work lay among the Picts and the Scots. Contact was also re-established with the Continent. Irish monks were prominent on the road to Rome, setting up their homes at Bobbio and Luxeuil and gaining reputation as teachers and students. The seventh century saw the culminating point in their work. From Iona through Lindisfarne they provided an important element in the conversion in depth of the pagan Anglo-Saxons. Roman discipline and organization gave the church in England its characteristic shape and order. Without Irish manpower it is hard to see how in the seventh century the conversion could have been achieved so successfully and peacefully. At the end of the seventh century the Northumbrian renaissance owed much to Irish influence and example.

All these achievements, in the mission field and in the cultural field, reacted upon the church in Ireland itself. Awareness of fellowship in great enterprise served as something of a social bond to the Irish. The nature of the enterprises drew the Irish away from political success. The abbeys flourished but native kingship decayed. Tribal institutions persisted, but loyalties were attracted more to the tribal monasteries rather than to the royal courts. Such strivings as there were towards larger political units were, if not negligible, at least restrained. A rough division was apparent between the north, including much of the west and centre, or the kingdom of Connaught, and the southern kingdom of Leinster, but men's natural loyalties passed (as in Wales) to the smaller groups, that can still be identified in place-names, into the men of Fermanagh, Monaghan, Armagh, Tyrone, or Derry. In such situations quarrels, sheep-stealing, cattle-raiding, and feuds over marriage arrangements were endemic. But, as far as we can see from the scanty and patchy records, the quarrels lacked the ferocity which characterized, for example, the Mercian campaigns against Kent or the Northumbrian civil wars of the same period. The wealth of the church, in spite of the closeness of tie between tribe and monastery, remained relatively untouched. It was not until the Viking rulers showed the way that the native Irish princes joined in, to make the ninth century one of the unhappiest in Ireland's history.

Political disunity and instability might well therefore have made Ireland a tempting prize for Viking enterprise. Yet awareness of the unity of the island was not completely lost and even received some institutional expression. Authority and physical power rested in the smaller units, but the concept of an *ard-ri*, a high king, persisted, and was given some air of reality by the recognition of a ruling line in the persons of the descendants of Niall of the Nine Hostages, a high king who flourished at the end of the fourth and beginning of the fifth centuries. The position of *ard-ri* was held by men claiming descent from Niall from the early fifth century to the opening years of the eleventh century. From 734 the northern and southern branches of the family enjoyed the honour in alternate succession. But only towards the end of the period did the high-kingship begin to indicate, let alone realise, its potentialities.

This rapid survey of the political state of the British Isles has been made with the object of showing how open the communities were to vigorous campaigning from outside. Only the English with their arable wealth had made serious strides towards unity, and there the sheer military weight of the Mercian house was breeding its own resistance. The Viking impact in its way forced unity upon the four main communities, but the shape of the political units in which the English, the Welsh, the Irish and the Scots would respectively predominate was by no means predetermined. Distortions, variations, peculiarities in what a racial or economic determinist would call the normal pattern abound. The direct reason for such so-called aberrations may often be attributed to the Norseman.

3

The course of the Scandinavian invasions to c. AD 954

The Viking Age lasted the best part of three centuries, and it is by no means easy to decide the most convenient and useful point to break a narrative account of the impact of the Northerners. Their aims, methods, and achievements varied from generation to generation and right to the end provide the historian with a complicated pattern of human nature and circumstance. There were settlers in the eighth century; there were raiders and pillagers in the eleventh. Active Danish, Norwegian and Swedish traders performed their more peaceful function throughout. Nevertheless if a break has to be made 954 represents as convenient a dividing point as any, marking as it does the end of the attempt to keep the north of England in a Scandinavian/Irish political orbit.

Within the first of these periods, c.786–954, each of the main communities suffered in different ways and at slightly different periods, interlocked and interdependent, and connected also with the ebb and flow of Viking invasion on the Continent, especially in Normandy. Scotland has been treated first because of a natural priority in time and also because of peculiarities in its development which make it essential to grasp the situation in the North if invasion elsewhere is to be understood. Ireland is treated next for a similar chronological reason, and Wales is brought into the story to round off the picture of events on the western seaboard of Britain. Last of all in place but not importance is England. Rather more than half this chapter will be taken up with English affairs not only because events are so much more fully recorded in relation to them, but also because truly decisive happenings not only for the British but for European history took place on English soil during these years.

Scotland

Scandinavian activity in Scotland concerned itself with three principal geographical areas: the Northern Isles, the Caledonian mainland, and the Western Isles extending as far as the Isle of Man. Most interesting and clearcut are the Northern Isles of Orkney and Shetland. These consist of two virtual archipelagos of islands, nearly 70 in the Orkneys and about 100 in the Shetlands, only comparatively few of which are now inhabited. Communications were of necessity by sea, and skilled seamen were needed to man the boats in what are often tempestuous and dangerous waters. Yet at several points in time these islands have been at the centre of important movements of people and civilization. Megalithic monuments such as the stone-built tomb of Maeshowe in Orkney, great henge monuments such as the Ring of Brodgar or the Ring of Bookan, the well-excavated and much discussed village site of Skara Brae, all testify to the vitality of the inhabitants of the islands in the two millennia BC. At a later stage the fantastic brochs, the stone-built tower of which at the best-known broch site at Clickhimin near Lerwick still stands 17 feet high, speak of a strong organized military community spreading from the mainland throughout the islands in the second and third centuries AD. Modern man is rightly amazed at the skill of the sailors of these periods from the Neolithic to the Early Iron Age. But though it is wrong to think of the islands as perpetually on the fringe of civilization, it is probably true to say that never were they as much at the centre of a great movement as during the Viking Age.

Mysteries surround the arrival of the Scandinavians in Orkney and Shetland. Both the state and nature of the original inhabitants and the date of the Scandinavian descent were even more a mystery to historians of the Middle Ages than they are now when there is still a deep division of opinion between those who claim evidence for strong pre-Viking contact between the Islands and Norway and those who insist that Norse settlement was not effective until well after AD 800. In Norway the *Historia Norwegiae* (dated to *c.*1200) took refuge in a set of good stories, describing the Picts as little more than pygmies, active builders in the morning and evening but hiding themselves in sheer terror in subterranean dwellings at midday when they lost all their strength. There were also Goidelic priests called *papae* because of their white robes. The medieval historians put natural emphasis on the deeds of Harold Fairhair and his followers, pirates of the kin of Ragnald, in the late ninth century. He is said to have established his winter quarters in the Orkneys from which summer forays were made, leading to the exercise of tyrannical rule now among the English, now the Scots, and now the Irish, to the point where they subjugated Northumbria in England, Caithness in Scotland, and Dublin and other seaports in Ireland.

Modern archaeological evidence tempers the emphasis on Harold Fairhair, proving Scandinavian presence in the islands from at least 800 and confirming the presence of Picts who were overwhelmed politically but not exterminated. Continuity in domestic building on sites such as Buckquoy in north-west Orkney suggest some element of cultural transmission. But well-authenticated and serious raids down the east and west coasts of Britain (*c.*786–840) become fully intelligible if associated with the presence of secure bases of the Jarlshof type in the Northern Isles, and one can postulate fairly a period of steady Scandinavian recruitment through the raiding period to about 865 or 870, followed by intense colonization coinciding with Harold Fairhair's activities late in the century. During this long period those of the original inhabitants who survived would be enslaved and lose their native social and Christian organization. Saga accounts substantiate the view of a predominantly heathen community in the Northern Isles as late as the early eleventh century.

All authorities agree that that heathen community was the direct product of a true migration, principally from Norway. Subtler linguistic work on dialect suggests a preponderance of settlers from the western fjords, especially from Rogaland and the *fylkir* to the south of Bergen. Remarkable excavations at Jarlshof, Sumbergh Head, the southernmost point of Shetland, have revealed characteristic features of an early Scandinavian settlement, the first elements of which are dated to the first half of the ninth century. A rectangular longhouse, some 70 feet by 20, with the longer walls curved in slightly at the ends, was the chief building. Beside the house itself there were outbuildings identified as a byre, a smithy and a bath-house. Animal bones and midden deposits suggest that farming activities predominated in this community – even fishing playing a relatively minor role. The presence of many stone loom-weights indicates the importance of textile activity. Bone combs, exquisitely carved pins with animal, axe-head and thistle decoration, speak of considerable artistic development. The peaceful nature of the settlement can probably be exaggerated. Virtual absence of weapons does not necessarily imply peace: rather it shows that the settlers took good care of their weapons and did not lose them. Later saga accounts refer to the settlers as ness-takers; men who, secure at sea, threw up hasty fortifications across the neck of a headland or peninsula to give themselves a base on land. Peaceful farming could come later when the settlement and land-taking were complete.

We know something of their institutions from Scandinavian analogies in the homeland and to some extent from archaeological and place-name evidence. The *bondi*, a peasant-farmer, represented the basic unit in society, head of a household with odal rights. Military leadership was supplied by sea-captains, but there is no evidence of an aristocratic principle at work, and no evidence for the transportation of rank over the North Sea except for the special respect shown to some men who may have been capable of boasting of royal blood in their veins. In the first settlement there was little room for the flourishing of lordly principles. We hear of men who styled themselves *jarl* but of no jarl (or earl) of Orkney or Shetland until the close of the ninth or beginning of the tenth century.

From their headquarters in the north, Scandinavians spread south to the mainland and west to the Western Isles in the course of the ninth and early tenth centuries. The first prominent ruler was Sigurd, brother of Ragnald Møre (and so probably the uncle of Rollo, first duke of Normandy) at the end of the ninth century. From the Orkney centre he exercised some authority over Shetland and also over Caithness. Place-names suggest Scandinavian penetration further south in Ross and Cromarty and Sutherland at the expense of Pictish power. The distribution of early Scandinavian names suggests that their movement was seaborne, that they established their little farming Jarlshof-type centres along the river valleys, relying on the rough pasture of the highland shielings to supplement and support the exiguous products of the poor barley-growing lands of the scanty lowlands. Whether they displaced or intermarried with the native population is uncertain, probably more of the latter than the former. The limit of Scandinavian penetration was indeterminate, far-reaching and longlasting in the modern shires as far south as the great spread of Inverness-shire, north of the great firth, no more than scattered, spasmodic, and temporary on the eastern seaboard of the Moray Firth and Aberdeenshire. The widest extent was probably reached as late as the middle of the eleventh century under the jarldom of Thorfinn the Mighty (d. 1065).

Expansion along the western coast of Scotland is more intelligible yet not easy to reconstruct in detail. The magnet was undoubtedly Ireland, but the trail of iron filings left scattered down to the Irish Sea, the Hebrides, Outer and Inner and the islands as far south as Man, must not be regarded as mere accidents of fate, refuges for those who had failed to reach their haven in Ireland. The islands had positive attractions for Scandinavian farmers and fishermen seeking a home and land for permanent settlement. Linguistic evidence suggests a degree of peaceful intermingling of Celtic and Scandinavian stocks. Archaeological evidence is scanty but sufficient to suggest an early accord between pagan newcomers and Christian inhabitants, and an early conversion to Christianity. In some places there was full continuity in the use of land. Christian cemeteries were used for pagan burials. Sculptural evidence is particularly strong in the Isle of Man to indicate that Celtic and Viking populations lived together in amity. A surprising number of Celtic names appear carved in Scandinavian runes. In an age when communications depended on the sea the islands continued to be treated as a unit, with two obvious geographical sub-units – the Nordreys and Sudreys. The notion of political allegiance to Norway continued to persist practically and actively in the north, to 1468-9, and strongly in the south to the middle of the thirteenth century.

Ireland

The pattern of Viking onslaught on Ireland is clear, though the detail is often obscure. Early raids between 795 and the 830 were followed by a period of intense settlement in fortified townships on the sea-coast. The key figures in the political events of this phase were the militant pagan Norwegian Thorgils (or Turgeis), a Norwegian chieftain of royal stock, Olaf of Dublin (c.857–71) and probably Ivar the Boneless, a Dane and the son of the Viking chieftain, Ragnar Lothbrok, whose death in Northumbria is said to have triggered off the main Viking attack on England in 865. During these middle years of the ninth century a Scandinavian presence in the harbours and ports of Ireland, especially in Dublin, was firmly established. A change comes over the pattern with the Scandinavian successes in England in the late 860s. From that time forward for the best part of a century the history of the Vikings in Ireland was inextricably mixed up with Viking enterprise in England, intimately and directly with enterprise in northern England. Larger Viking ambitions ended in failure. The sons of Ivar and his grandsons were constantly active and often formidable, but they failed to establish a permanent dynasty. Dublin and York, the two twin power centres of their family – and of other Viking families too – were sometimes for brief periods brought under the rule of one man but more often went their own paths. The Irish Sea which the Vikings dominated for decades proved inadequate as a reservoir of political strength. The return of Olaf Cuaran, son of Sihtric, from York to Dublin in 952, followed by the eclipse of the Scandinavian kingdom of York itself in 954 put an end to the most extravagant of Scandinavian aims in Britain.

Wider Viking ambitions, conspicuously expressed in attempts to create a living kingdom of York and Dublin but not confined to English ventures, had an important bearing on native Irish history. The Scandinavian impact was tremendous but the danger of the complete Scandinavianization of Ireland was lessened considerably by these wider preoccupations. In the event the first long phase of Scandinavian attack left the mainland of Ireland overwhelmingly in Irish hands. The dominant note in Viking settlement was more attuned to the sea than to the land, the typical creation the fortified port with dependent hinterland, not the cluster of farms of the Scottish Islands. More often than not within Ireland itself the Vikings appeared as yet another element in the inter-tribal warfare of Ireland, now allying with the men of the North, now with the Southerners, now fighting in unison, now among themselves, Dane against Norwegian or Norwegian against Norwegian.

Detailed record of political events is spasmodic and at times ambiguous. The 790s, which had seen the sack of Lindisfarne, also saw Viking disaster strike the monks of Iona and the monks settled on the island of Lambey north of Dublin off the Leinster coast. In 795 Northmen sailing south from Skye, possibly the same group that had found Iona a profitable target, plundered and burnt the church at Lambey in the first recorded attack on Irish soil. For close on forty years sporadic raids on ill-defended monasteries continued to harass the Irish, though as certain scholars have been quick to point out not all the raiding and destruction should be attributed to Northern sources. These early Viking attacks seems to have coincided with a loss of moral force among the Christian Irish themselves. Churches and monasteries which for centuries had been regarded as sacrosanct became the prey of Irish ravagers as well as of Norse. At some time in the 830s raiding gave way to permanent settlement associated with the shadowy and heroic figure of the pagan Norwegian prince Thorgils, or Turgeis. He seems to have made the North his political centre after the capture of Armagh, but under his tutelage if not always under his direct protection Norwegians set up their coastal strongholds at Anagassan on the coast of Louth, Waterford, Wexford, and most important of all at Dublin. The open Atlantic held no terrors for the Norwegians. They set up a small settlement on the Shannon at Limerick and, almost incredibly, at a later date even attacked the savage, isolated and one would imagine virtually impregnable, rock islet monastery of Skellig Michael, eight miles from the coast of Kerry, towering, almost sheer, cliff high above the turbulent and treacherous Atlantic. Thorgils, an intense pagan, roused Christian feeling against him, and was captured and drowned by his enemies in 845. Olaf of Dublin and Ivar the Boneless and his successors sustained and strengthened what were virtually pirate bases, particularly Dublin with its fine commanding position on the Irish Sea. There was no serious attempt whatsoever to conquer Ireland. In this phase of Viking impact on Ireland right the way through to Olaf Cuaran's failure at York in 951, Scandinavian ambitions, Norwegian and Danish, were concentrated on the ports which they themselves constructed and fortified. They provided a constant irritant to the Irish political body, dabbling in tribal politics, creating a new Irish/Scandinavian society only in their fortified townships on the coast, acting at times openly as mercenaries. Under provocation Cearbhall, the native king of Leinster, sacked Dublin in 902 and it took the concerted efforts of a new Scandinavian attack under Ragnald (Rægnvold), the grandson of Ivar, in the second decade of the tenth century, to re-establish the Viking coastal hold from Waterford to Dublin, setting up what was virtually a new planned town at Dublin itself. Ireland was treated as something of a milch-cow, a source of supply of slaves for use in colonizing schemes elsewhere, notably in Iceland, and as the essential base and haven for attacks on England and Wales. One of the reasons why the story of Scandinavian attacks on Britain appears at times in the records to have been so scrappy and uncoordinated is because so little is said of the steady recouping, refurbishing, and re-equipping that was the special function of the Irish strongholds, notably Dublin, in this massive enterprise. It is probable that as many Viking attacks were launched east from Dublin as south from Orkney, and virtually certain that more came immediately east from the Irish ports than direct from Norway.

Wales

The Welsh by reason of geography, favourable political accident, and possibly because of their relative poverty, weathered the Viking attacks in the period c.790–950 with surprising success. Danish attacks in the 790s were repulsed with heavy loss and later attacks in the 850s and 860s appear to have been little more than probing raids on the lowlands of Gower and Anglesey, part and parcel of the general unrest which was to culminate in the main onslaught against England in 865. Wales does not provide a good coastline for hostile forces to attack. The fine sandy beaches of Anglesey, Pembrokeshire and Gower, are more than countered by difficulties of approach, treacherous currents, and uncertain winds.

The indirect effect of Scandinavian pressure was undoubtedly great. In the ninth century Rhodri Mawr, prince of Gwynedd, 844–78, maintained the integrity of his principality in spite of serious attempts to set up Scandinavian settlements in Anglesey. He defeated and killed the Danish leader Gorm in what seems to have been a campaign of more than usual importance in 855. Even so, for a short while in the last years of his reign he was forced, after defeats at the hands of the Danes, to seek exile in Ireland. Anglesey was again attacked in the early tenth century, first by Vikings suffering from Irish victories at Dublin in 902 and later in consequence of the general surge of Viking activity in the Irish Sea area after 914. Neither attack was completely successful, the first diverted to Chester and so opening up an important stage in the settlement of north-west England, the second no more than a giant raid, a by-product of Viking restoration of their hold on Irish ports. South Wales was subject to greater strains. Pembrokeshire, offering a long and easy line of entry through Milford Haven, suffered sporadic attack and possible limited settlement along the Haven. The recoil of the remnants of the great hordes which failed to crush Alfred's Wessex led to severe raiding to the north as well as to the south of the Severn Sea. In 914, as part and parcel of intensified Viking activity, and possibly in direct consequence of the settlement of Normandy, a Viking host from Brittany, led by the two earls, Ohter and Hroald, ravaged the Welsh coast and penetrated the Wye Valley as far as Archenfield where they captured Bishop Cyfeiliog, bishop of Llandaff. The bishop was ransomed for £40 by the English king. Native developments in the south as well as the north helped to safeguard Wales. One of the greatest of medieval Welsh rulers,

Hywel Dda, Hywel the Good, flourished during the first half of the tenth century. He was a close friend of the West Saxon dynasty, worked well in harmony with them, and cooperated fully in meeting the Scandinavian menace which afflicted Christian Wales and England alike. About 920 he consolidated his hold on south-west Wales by campaigns in Pembrokeshire which may have had the effect of limiting Viking activity in that sensitive area. By 942 he was virtually master of all Wales. From the first long drawn-out phase of Scandinavian attack Wales appeared to have emerged without mortal wound and indeed strengthened. Hywel had protected the Welsh people and offered prospect of a greater unity very much as Alfred and his successors had offered protection and prospects to the West Saxon and the English.

England

English affairs are better recorded than affairs in the Celtic world with the result that we can follow at times in great detail the ebb and flow of Scandinavian attack on England. The overall pattern is quite clear. Raids in the later part of the eighth century were followed by a period of calm, broken in the 830s. The correspondence with events in Ireland is striking, but the English were wealthier, stronger, and better equipped to stand the initial strain. Their resistance was successful and the Danes did not winter in England until the year 850–1. From that point onwards however the momentum of attack grew, and serious colonization started in 865 with a climax reached about the year 878 when Alfred, king of Wessex, succeeded in checking the Danish advance. During the last decades of the century an uneasy political truce was established, leaving the Danes in command of most of England to the east and north of Watling Street and the river Lea, and the house of Wessex in substantial command of unconquered Christian England. Norwegian/Irish penetration of the north west intensified in the early part of the tenth century but an attempt to set up a straggling trading-based kingdom of Dublin and York failed. Under the leadership of a series of capable kings, greater Wessex re-absorbed the Danish-held territories so that by 954 the political shape of a unified Christian or Christianized England was fully formed.

In a famous entry (for 789) the Anglo-Saxon Chronicle records the first coming of the Vikings to England during the reign of

King Brihtric (786–802). Three boatloads of Norwegians from Hörthaland arrived off the Dorset coast. A king's reeve, apparently under the impression that they were traders, tried to force them to come to the king's residence. He himself had been stationed at Dorchester. The Norsemen turned on him and killed the reeve and his men. Four years later the Chronicle records the fearsome sack of the monastery at Lindisfarne and we are given the well-attested date of 8 June 793 for this event. Further ravaging (not without loss) is reported from Northumbria in 794 at the monastery of *Donemuthan*, presumably Jarrow/Wearmouth. A feature of these entries, reinforced by the voluminous correspondence which passed between England and the Frankish court of Charles the Great on the subject of the sack of Lindisfarne, is the completely unexpected nature of these happenings. The reeve at Dorchester had expected to find peaceful traders on the Dorset coast, men from within the civilized world, who would subscribe to the customs and conventions of the community and who would go peacefully with their goods to the royal residence. Alcuin writing from Charles's court to the Northumbrian king gives the best insight into the shock and horror with which the sack of Lindisfarne was greeted throughout the Christian world.

> Lo, it is nearly 350 years that we and our fathers have inhabited this most lovely land, and never before has such terror appeared in Britain as we have now suffered from a pagan race, nor was it thought that such an inroad from the sea could be made. Behold the church of St Cuthbert spattered with the blood of the priests of God, despoiled of all its ornaments; a place more venerable than all in Britain is given as a prey to pagan people. (*English Historical Documents* i (1979) no. 193)

It was natural for Alcuin to look for an inner explanation of these happenings, to attribute them to sin, to fornication, avarice, robberies, even to the dress, the way of wearing the hair, the luxurious habits of the princes and people. The good Northumbrians are exhorted to look to their trimming of beard and hair, in which they have wished to ape the pagan. And the lesson is made plain when Alcuin writes: 'What should be expected for other places, when the divine judgment has not spared this holy place?'

These early raids were Norwegian and were accompanied by, and possibly a product of, sporadic settlement in the islands to the north and west of Britain. The Danes were also active, stirred up, as some observers thought, by the ferment which resulted from the creation of the great Frankish Empire by Charles the Great. Reduction of the independence of continental Saxony and Frisia contributed to native Danish unrest. But for the first thirty years or so of the ninth century most Danish turbulence seemed to be directed against fellow Danes. Not until the 830s was a substantial proportion of Danish energy unleashed against the Western world. England now became a prime target for their unwelcome attentions.

The Anglo-Saxon Chronicle, which was put together in the form we know it in the 890s, becomes our chief source of information concerning the Scandinavian attacks. Supplemented at times by entries in continental chronicles it provides a picture of constant attack or threat of attack throughout the ninth century. In 835 a heavy raid was directed against the Isle of Sheppey. The east and south east continued during this phase of onslaught to bear the brunt of piratical raids. The pirates went where the wealth was greatest. Twice, in 850 in the Isle of Thanet, and in 854 in Sheppey, there is record of Danish armies wintering in England. Throughout the whole thirty years to 865 there is however, no clearcut attempt at permanent colonization. This generation was concerned with loot and sporadic raids rather than systematic probing of defences with a view to stable settlement.

Danish ambitions during the last third of the ninth century were of a very different nature. The moment of change came in autumn 865. An army, described by the Chronicle as large, landed in East Anglia. Its leadership was principally in the hands of the sons of Ragnar Lothbrok, or Leather-Breeches, especially Ivar the Boneless and Healfden and Ubba. It would be wrong, however, to suggest unified command. There were many kings and earls with the Danish host. It is highly probable that the most meaningful element in the leadership was the personal authority of the sea-captains who commanded the individual longships and the warriors who sailed in them. A captain of royal blood would be known as a king and might exert loose authority over a small fleet; a powerful captain, again possibly exercising authority over a small fleet, might from past rank and present power be known as earl (*jarl*). They operated as armies in face of strong native reaction. The ferocity of their attacks is proven by all manner of evidence: for example, exact work on the deposit of coin hoards in England has proved beyond doubt that a substantial peak occurred in the deposit of hoards during the decade 865–75. Their army organization persisted to some measure as conquest gave place to settlement. But always underneath the facade of regional unity existed the independence of the smaller group, the ships' crews that continued to give protection as further immigrants settled and intensified the Danish hold on a large section of northern and eastern England.

The political story of the succeeding years is intimately bound up with the career of King Alfred of Wessex, the one Christian leader with the strength and will to check the Danish hosts. From 865 to 871, the year of battles in the course of which Alfred succeeded to the West Saxon throne, Danish victories were continuous. They used East Anglia as their base for supply and recruitment from the autumn of 865 to the autumn of 866. Extensive damage to Thetford, and some evidence for incendiarism in the cathedral of North Elmham may have occurred at this stage. The Danes were especially anxious to equip themselves with horses and it was as a mounted host that they embarked on the conquest of Northumbria in 866–7, in the course of which the great monastery at Whitby was sacked. York itself was captured on 21 March. Northumbria had been weakened by a civil war in which King Osbert had been rejected by his people who had chosen Aella, a man not of the royal stock, and the reputed slayer of Ragnar, as their king. The Vikings found such a situation to their taste, wintered at York, and after Osbert and Aella in a temporary reluctant reconciliation were both killed in a partially successful attack on the city, the Vikings appear to have set up an English prince who exercised nominal rule there *sub potestate Danorum*. The Danes then wintered at Nottingham, after ravaging Mercia and forcing the Mercian king Burgred to buy peace from them. In the autumn of 868 they descended again on York and the following year they moved back into East Anglia, defeating and killing the East Anglian king Edmund (855–69), who was quickly honoured as a saint and martyr by his countrymen. His death, probably as a captive in Danish hands, on 20 November 869, is immensely important. It marks the end of native Christian kingship in East Anglia. The impact on the Scandinavians themselves was also to prove formidable; in the twelfth century the conversion of Iceland was dated 1000 years after the birth of our Lord and 130 after the death of king Edmund. Northumbria also fell completely under Danish control though for the time being Egbert, a puppet Englishman, bore the royal title. The time was now ripe for a trial of strength with the strongest surviving English kingdom, the kingdom of Wessex.

From the autumn of 870 to King Alfred's death in 899, the dominant political theme was indeed the struggle between the West
Saxons and the Danes. When the campaign opened Alfred was not
yet king. He was the *secundarius*, the young heir-apparent to his
brother King Ethelred, 22 or 23 years of age. The Danes moved their
army headquarters to Reading and for a solid twelvemonth strove
to break West Saxon resistance. This year of battles saw victories on
both sides. Danish checks at Englefield and Ashdown (where one
Danish king and five earls were killed) were followed by English
reverses at Basing and *Meretun*. King Ethelred died in April 871 and
Alfred succeeded. English defeats at Reading and Wilton forced the
new king to buy peace from the Danes who were now in secure control of the Thames estuary and of London. But Alfred had at the
least preserved his own authority over the West Saxons.

Alfred's reign may be divided conveniently into three clearly
defined political and military phases. For the first seven years the
Danes held the full initiative and it was much in the balance whether
or not the whole of England would fall into their grasp. The middle
years of the reign, from 878 to 891, were period of consolidation and
of the marking out of new though in the event impermanent political
frontiers. During the last eight years from 891 to 899, the last serious
threat came of a political conquest of Wessex, a threat which came
to an end with the break up of the 'great horde', the *micel here* as
the Chronicle called it, in the summer of 896. It is customary to read
this epic story from the defenders' point of view. Undoubtedly
Alfred was a great king and his achievements played a dominant
part in the shaping of a united Christian monarchy in England. He
preserved Christian Wessex as a nucleus of a united England. He
heightened the idea of a Christian monarchy by precept and example. It is salutary on occasions, however, to look at the political
situation from the other point of view. Concentration on English
resilience and awareness of ultimate English political success should
not lead to neglect of Danish achievement and permanent social
success. From 871 to 878 the Danish armies extended their hold
in depth over East Anglia, Northumbria and the greater part of
Mercia. Their 'great army' overwintered in 873–4 at Repton where
archaeologists have discovered sensational evidence of their presence: possible ritual burial of a great Viking chief, and slip-ways for
ships, a virtual charnel house of bones from well over two hundred
bodies. They inflicted a decisive defeat on the Mercian king Burgred
in 874. They initiated, under the leadership of Healfden, an agrarian

settlement in Northumbria in 876. They effected a rough partition of Mercia in 877. The following year, 878, was the year of decision. The Danes under the command of Guthrum overran the greater part of Wessex, forced Alfred to take refuge in the marshes of Athelney, and came within an ace of achieving complete conquest. King Alfred's emergence from Athelney, his rallying of his warrior-thegns and victory at Edington brought this phase of Danish onslaught to its conclusion. The Treaty of Wedmore between Alfred and Guthrum was followed by the conversion of Guthrum to Christianity. From the Christian West Saxon point of view Edington and Wedmore have intelligibly been interpreted as a saving mercy. This is not the only possible point of view. The terms of Wedmore did nothing to loosen the hold of the Danish armies on territories they had already occupied. Indeed Guthrum's army remained quartered in Chippenham throughout the summer of 878. Only in the autumn did they withdraw to Cirencester in English Mercia and not until 879 did they withdraw east to embark on a systematic settlement of East Anglia. The Danes could pride themselves on having won recognition now within the Christian community itself. The settlement in some ways represented a legitimization of their authority, though the situation was probably not completely clarified until 885-6. The boundary between Danish dominated England and English England lay through the old kingdom of Mercia in a line running roughly from north west to south east, from Chester along Watling Street to the river Lea and so to London. This boundary between what was later known as the Danelaw and English England became a permanent feature of the social and institutional life of these islands. London remained, temporarily it is true, in Danish hands. The campaigning, season of 878 had resulted in a military defeat at Edington, but the Danish army remained essentially intact and formidable. Its leader, Guthrum, was strengthened rather than weakened by his baptism. The attempted conquest of Wessex had failed, but attractive possibilities were now open in the east free from fear of West Saxon interference, and to some measure in accord with West Saxon wishes. The Chronicle records carefully that in 879 Guthrum, now a Christian king who took on the baptismal name of Athelstan, shared out the land in East Anglia. The kingdom of St Edmund had passed into Danish but not into heathen hands. It is possible, given their likely limitation in manpower and their assumed ambitions to win land for farming, that the Treaty of Wedmore gave the Danes of this first invasion precisely what they themselves wanted, an opportunity to regularize their own territorial settlement in the North and East.

The middle years of Alfred's reign following the Treaty of Wedmore to the arrival of the great host from the Continent in 891 represent a working out of the consequences of the political movements of the 870s. Guthrum died in 890 and on the whole upheld the promises to keep the peace which he had sworn to his godfather, King Alfred, during the baptismal ceremonies of 878. Alfred made one formidable advance in 886 when he occupied London. This was part of a move to free the Thames estuary from further piracy and was further associated with internal English political happenings. We are told by the Chronicle in connection with the move on London that the English people who were not under subjection to the Danes submitted to him, and further that he entrusted the borough to the control of the ealdorman Ethelred. Alfred was now the sole surviving ruling prince of the old royal stocks and it was natural that the surviving English authorities should look to him. The ealdorman Ethelred, was a Mercian who quickly became if he was not so already – the date of the marriage is uncertain – Alfred's own son-in-law. He and his wife Aethelflæd, later known as the Lady of the Mercians, are crucial figures in the successful attempt to bring the West Saxons and the English Mercians into peaceful union. The issue of what was to be the most attractive type of silver penny of Alfred's later reign, a coin with the London monogram inscribed on the reverse, undoubtedly dates from 886. The principal Danish endeavours in fact seem during the 880s to have been directed towards continental Europe. One of the great difficulties of dealing with a period as fluid politically as the ninth century consists precisely in the complicated interaction of movements of these very mobile Scandinavians on the various more settled communities of the West. Within the area that we can now conveniently call the Danelaw consolidation of agrarian settlement and retention of military organization are both apparent. Land settlement and the introduction of immigrants were achieved under the discipline of armies which maintained fortified headquarters at Northampton, Cambridge, Tempsford, Thetford and Huntingdon. The 'five boroughs' of the north-east Midlands, Leicester, Nottingham, Derby, Lincoln and Stamford, were probably fortified effectively at this time, a preparatory step to urbanization. In the north, York dominated the whole area, rapidly developing into a powerful Scandinavian fortified market, comparable with Dublin in its commercial aspects and more important than Dublin in that York also emerged as the political heart of a vigorous colonizing movement in Northumbria. Evidence from the later histories of the see of St Cuthbert at Durham, coupled with possible interpretation of the coin evidence, suggests a succession of kings at York prepared to work with the archbishops (Archbishop Wulfhere who was prominent in the early crises of the 870s was still active in the early 890s). Guthfrith, who may well have become the outstanding Viking leader in 880 after Healfden's death, enjoyed a good reputation among Christian historians, possibly because of the part he played in the transfer of the see at Lindisfarne to Chester-le-Street, and was buried in August 895 at his head church, presumably the cathedral at York. Excavations at York have been enough to suggest a strong trading community at a very early stage. By 891 a whole mass of Scandinavian and Anglo-Scandinavian communities were established in the Danelaw. Some of the Vikings had been settled in their own farms or urban dwellings at York for half a generation and more. Some retained their native paganism but others had followed the example of Guthrum and Guthfrith and had accepted Christianity. Stone carving and sculpture for example in the Vale of Pickering, especially at Middleton, indicates a coming together of Christian and pagan motifs at a very early stage in the settlement of Yorkshire, probably from this very generation. Excavations at York Minster, too, have yielded evidence of continuity in stone-carving and epigraphic usage. For a people with no native coinage the Scandinavians took early to the use of coins. Already by the last decade of the late ninth century coins were struck in Danish-occupied England, some by English moneyers recruited specially to York and to East Anglia where religious motifs and inscriptions on the coins indicate the intensity of religious beliefs in new converts. Not all can have welcomed the new irruption of Scandinavian despoilers which came to afflict England in the 890s.

The troubles of the 890s were a direct consequence of the stiffening of continental resistance to Danish attack. The successful defence of Paris 886–7 was followed by Arnulf's victory at the battle of the river Dyle (near Louvain) in 891. At some time between September 891 and September 892 a force of 250 ships sailed from Boulogne, carrying their horses with them, landing at the estuary of the river Lympne in south-east Kent. Alfred's defensive measures were still incomplete and the half-built, poorly defended fortress at or near Appledore was swiftly overrun. Danish reinforcements under Haesten set up a further camp at Milton in north-east Kent. The details of the campaigns of the following three years were carefully preserved by a contemporary witness. The strategic heart of the matter is clear enough. Formidable Danish armies from their sea-protected fortified bases in Kent and Essex, north and south of the Thames estuary, with intermittent help from the already settled Danes in East Anglia and Northumbria, attempted to overthrow Alfred's kingdom. They failed. Organization and systematic defence defeated them. A ring of fortified *burhs* (for the most part well-fortified townships) proved an effective shield for Wessex itself. The loyalty and courage of subordinate ealdormen, and of Alfred's son Edward and his son-in-law, Ethelred of Mercia, contributed to Danish defeat. They ravaged deep along the Thames valley, along the Severn valley and into Wales. But in 896 the enterprise was abandoned, the great horde split up, and the Chronicle was able accurately to sum the situation up, recording that 'by the grace of God the army had not on the whole afflicted the English people very greatly'. Alfred's last three years, 896 to his death on 26 October 899, were spent in peace.

The last Danish campaigns which failed are in their way as instructive as the earlier campaigns which succeeded. Women and children were present at the Danish camps in Benfleet. The armies were as ready poised for successful settlement in the 890s as their fathers and kinsfolk had been in the 60s and 70s. They did not succeed in winning a patrimony for themselves in south-east England, let alone Wessex and English Mercia. Not until the successful French campaigns of 911 and 912 twenty years later, was territory opened for primarily Danish settlement in what was to become the Duchy of Normandy. Yet a genuine land-hunger existed and a genuine land-hunger was in fact assuaged. The Chronicle tells us that with the disruption of the great army those who had enough property and money bought themselves into the settled communities of Danish East Anglia and Northumbria. No better example could be given both of the success and of the limitations of Alfred's policy. The integrity of English England was preserved. The strength of the settled Scandinavian population, capable of buying and selling land in company with fellow-Scandinavian and English farmers, was increased and intensified in the Danelaw.

The main interest of the second half of the ninth century consists within these islands in the survival of a strong kingdom of Wessex, the nucleus of a kingdom of England, and the provision in the

Danelaw of opportunity under temporary Scandinavian military lordship for more concentrated agrarian settlement. This was primarily a Danish venture. Skills learned in the harder but not utterly unsuitable environment of Jutland, Funen and Zealand could be employed to greater advantage in the possibly under-populated lands of some parts of Lincolnshire, Yorkshire, East Anglia, and the territory of the Five Boroughs. The first half of the tenth century saw the reabsorption of these territories under English lordship. Time was given in the critical forty years between the Treaty of Wedmore 878 and the decisive campaigns of Alfred's son which reaches a climax in 918 for a whole generation of Danish farmers to be accepted as a permanent and peaceful feature of the landscape of north and east England.

The story of the reconquest of the Danelaw is complicated, partly because it is in the nature of reabsorption. Danish farmers, settled and often Christianized, came to realize that their best hope of peaceful future lay in acceptance of the overlordship of the West Saxon dynasty. A succession of able kings, building further on Alfred's work, showed the right combination of military strength, planning ability, and political sense to bring success to the dynasty. Under Edgar 959–75, a truly united Christian kingdom of England came into being. The progress to such an end was not smooth, nor should it be regarded as inevitable. Vicious cross-currents from Ireland and the Isles – not so much from the Continent, and little direct from Denmark or Norway – tormented the political scene. Under Edward, 899–924, English political authority was reasserted over Eastern Mercia and East Anglia. His son and successor, the brilliant Athelstan, prematurely brought the whole of Northumbria under his control and was widely recognized throughout the British world. The twenty years after his death in 939 was a period of vacillating fortune, complicated by the success of the Norwegian and Irish adventurers in Dublin and York. After 954 the situation eased and Edgar's triumphant and peaceful reign (959–75) may rightly be interpreted as a fitting climax to this hard century of Christian resistance and Danish attack.

From the Scandinavian point of view two features are of outstanding importance. The first of these is the largely unchronicled but firmly evidenced fact of Norwegian-Irish settlement in the north west of England. The second, a tribute to the success of the Danish farmer rather than the Danish soldier, is the acceptance within the new Christian kingdom of England of a special law, special customs, special agrarian institutions. Both features owed much to tensions within the Scandinavian world itself, to the commercial success which attended the opening up of the regular route from Dublin to York and which should not be masked by the ultimate political failure of the Norwegians at York, and to the fear which developed on the part of the more settled Danish colonists of the earlier generations for the more mobile Norwegian-Irish traders and raiders of the later generations. The settlers accepted Christianity quickly. Two of the outstanding clerics of the first half of the tenth century had powerful contacts with the Danelaw. Theodred, bishop of London, 926–51, effectively looked after much of the East Anglian kingdom. Oda, archbishop of Canterbury, 941–58, was himself of Danish birth and said to be a son of a Dane who came to England with the early settlers. He showed lively interest in the Fenland country, interceding with the king on behalf of a Cambridgeshire thegn, and receiving land at Ely. His nephew, St Oswald, a son of Oda's brother, continued the family interest in land and church affairs in the Danelaw. Heathenism does not appear to have retained a firm hold on the Scandinavians. Even in the North Riding of Yorkshire only one certain heathen place-name – Roseberry Topping – has been identified. Further south an Edgar the Peaceful was more to the taste of the Danish colonists of the Five Boroughs than an Eric Bloodaxe.

In the reign of Edward the Elder the first firm steps were taken towards the reabsorption of the Danes. Permanent fortifications at strategic points were established throughout western Mercia very much in line with Alfred's West Saxon defensive policy. A series of campaigns in 917 and 918 resulted in the seizing of Derby, an English victory at Tempsford and the rapid reduction or capitulation of the remaining Danish armies south of the Humber. Moves were even made by the Scandinavians in York to submit to Aethlflæd, sister of Edward the Elder. Her death on 12 June 918 brought these moves to a fruitless end. But by the end of the year after the surrender of Nottingham all the people settled in Mercia, including apparently the men of Lincoln, submitted to King Edward. The West Saxon king in 919 spent his best energies ensuring his own peaceful succession to Mercia and in the meantime Ragnald, the Viking leader from Dublin, successfully contended for a kingdom in York. The Anglo-Saxon Chronicle, its natural sympathies heightened by the drama of events, treats 920 as an *annus mirabilis*, and tells us that in this year there submitted to King Edward the Scottish king and people,

Ragnald of York, the native ealdorman, Ealdred of Bamborough, with all the Northumbrians, English, Danish, Northmen, and others – and the king and people of Strathclyde. Welsh princes are also said to have submitted to him and to have paid homage to him. Undoubtedly the Chronicler has seized on the poetry of the situation. Alfred's son was widely recognized as overlord. Modern historians, while paying tribute to his achievements, have been more sceptical of the realities of his power. Constant effort was needed to preserve the union of Mercia and Wessex. In the last year of his reign Edward had to deal with a rebellion of Mercians in alliance with Welsh princes focused on Chester. There was nothing he could do north of the Humber. Danish political independence to the south of that river had been destroyed. Ragnald, by gaining formal recognition from Edward, had intruded a new potentially dangerous element into English politics.

Meanwhile under cover of all the political battles and the fortifications of Chester, of Thelwall, of Runcorn, of Bakewell, the last of the serious colonization ventures in England was under way. Place-names are our best guide and inference from cultural development, notably in stone sculpture, also adds to our knowledge. Substantial settlement of an Irish-Norwegian population, men and women from the Scandinavian ports in Ireland, from the Isle of Man, and from the Scottish islands, took place in north-west England. A great hoard of coins deposited at Cuerdale in Lancashire in the earliest years of the century, probably in AD 903, gives evidence of the trader-raider moves that went on between Dublin and York side by side with the colonization. There is a vast quantity of Viking-style sculpture in the north of England, much of it (such as the Dacre and Gosforth crosses) exhibiting clear signs of Hiberno-Norse inspiration, though some shows traits suggesting more direct contact with the Scandinavian homeland. Land not utterly dissimilar to the native Norwegian territory in the Lake District and surrounding territories proved more attractive to men of ultimate Scandinavian descent than to the Anglo-Saxons. In many of the deep valleys of Cumberland and Westmorland the place-name structure suggests that Irish-Scandinavian farmers met a British people with little or no Saxon admixture. The low-lying territories are different; and there in Lancashire and further north around the Solway Firth there is plentiful sign of early Saxon settlement. But over much of Cumberland, Westmorland, north Lancashire and west Yorkshire a vital new element was added to the ethnic pattern in the early decades of the tenth century during the reign of Edward the Elder.

English impotence north of the Humber also threatened at one stage the intrusion and reinforcement of powerful Scandinavian elements in the north east. A later writer, anxious to establish the history of the see of St Cuthbert, relates how Ragnald, king of the Vikings at Waterford (probably the same Ragnald who ruled at York after 919), won victories north of the Tees, dividing out the conquered territory among his chief soldiers, two of whom are mentioned by name, Scula, who was given an extensive tract roughly 100 square miles or so in extent between the modern Castle Eden and Billingham while Olaf Ball (who is said to have sworn oaths by Thor and by Odin) received a similar massive grant from Castle Eden to the mouth of the Wear. Sir Frank Stenton, who first noted the true importance of these references as descriptions of precise settlement arrangements, pointed out the similarity in extent of the grants to some of the later sokes of the Danelaw, that is to say, areas over which the landlord exercised special rights of jurisdiction, such as Bolingbroke in Lincolnshire. The arrangement seems to have been reached between 912 and 915, and involved the transmission of clear political and military overlordship. There was not the same intensity of land-taking at this stage by the Irish-Norse elements in the north east as in the north west.

Edward's son and successor, Athelstan, 924–39, is remembered as one of the most powerful and spectacular rulers of the dynasty. He had been brought up in Mercia, was readily accepted as king by the Mercians and did more than any other single ruler to bring about by inspiration and deed a true union of West Saxon and Mercian. He strengthened contacts with the Welsh and had little difficulty in expelling the Scandinavians from York in 927. In European affairs he was widely known and respected. Harold Fairhair, king of Norway, treated with him as settled king to settled king, sent a great warship 'with golden prow and purple sail, armed within by a dense row of gilded shields' to Athelstan as a personal present, and permitted his youngest son, Haakon, Athelstan's foster-son, to be brought up at Athelstan's court. Although Athelstan's most enduring contribution to the unity of England came in connection with the imposition of effective royal government on southern England he is chiefly remember for his victory at Brunanburh in 937. A full poetic account of the battle was incorporated in the Anglo-Saxon Chronicle. It represented a great victory for the Christian English, led by Athelstan and his young brother Edmund, against a coalition of Scots, British and Scandinavian Irish. The foremost leader and indeed creator of the coalition was Olaf Guthfrithson, the son of the man Athelstan had expelled from York in 927. Olaf survived to take his tattered remnant of an army back to Dublin, but no fewer than five men of royal rank and seven earls were killed from Ireland alone. Brunanburh inflicted a sharp check to the political ambitions of the Irish Scandinavian community.

The check proved, however, to be temporary only. With the death of Athelstan in 939 came fresh opportunity. By the end of the year Olaf Guthfrithson was back in York. In 940 he threatened to undo the work of the preceding generation and by a treaty drawn up by the two archbishops of York and Canterbury gained possession of the whole of the Danelaw. His death and the succession of lesser men, his cousin Olaf Sihtricson and his brother Ragnald Guthfrithson in turn destroyed this arrangement. For the last years of Edmund's reign, 944–6, the West Saxon house was again in political control of the North. But a further period of confusion and doubt followed Edmund's assassination in 946. Eric 'Bloodaxe' of Norway, a son of Harold Fairhair, Olaf Sihtricson of Dublin (949–52), and finally for two years Eric again (952–4) ruled at York. The Northumbrians themselves drove him out. His subsequent death at Stainmore brings a symbolic end to this phase of the history of northern England. Eadred, Edmund's successor, played little active part in the final events. Lack of single-minded purpose after the death of Olaf Guthfrithson contributed to the failure of the Irish Scandinavians to set up a permanent political hold on Dublin and York. The intrusion of a formidable and ambitious native Norwegian prince in the person of Eric Bloodaxe underlined the fluidity and complexity of the situation. The hard work inside the southern English kingdoms, the provision of better peace, the identification of Christianized Danish farmers with the surviving Christian dynasty helped to ensure that the future hope of a peaceful kingdom rested on the House of Wessex. Yet the time factor alone – the simple chronology of settlement of Dane in east and Norwegian/ Irish in north west – helped to bring it about that the united England of Edgar's reign was a more complex ethnic entity than the familiar Heptarchic pattern of Wessex, Mercia, Northumbria and East Anglia.

4

Scandinavia during the later stages of the Viking Age, c.954–c.1100

The first long phase of the Viking movement was a colonizing phase with settlement and consolidation of settlement heavily concentrated in the later ninth and early tenth centuries. The North, after 954, continued to be active for a further century and more. Yet the raids and torments inflicted on the West were essentially different from those of the earlier period, increasingly so as the eleventh century progressed.

Acceptance of Christianity is the key to the situation, the dividing line between civilized and barbarian. Colonists living in Christian communities accepted Christianity as a condition of permanence. Viking leaders with ambitions to set up permanent dynasties found it expedient, at times essential, to profess adherence to Christianity. At home in Scandinavia kings discovered the advantages of a literate universal faith to support them in imposing government on peoples where paganism and localism were ready companions. Conversion did not necessarily involve savage rejection of all the attributes of the old religion: paganism lingered on in out-of-the-way places, tolerated and ineffective. By the third quarter of the eleventh century Scandinavia was substantially integrated into Christendom. Pope Gregory VII (1073–85), could exercise his ideal of papal supremacy in Nidaros, Roskilde, and Lund as well as to the Germano-Roman heartlands of the Carolingian and Ottonian empires.

Denmark became the most important unit in Scandinavia during the last Viking century, though its rise to political prominence was quite sudden, associated with the establishment of a more stable agrarian base and possible improvements in ploughing techniques and control of arable wealth. The development of towns and fortresses, bridge-building, better communications, the greater use of stone in construction become visible evidence of renewal together with the dramatic implications of the adoption of Christianity and a native coinage. The key figure was King Harold Bluetooth (*c.*945–*c.*985).The Danish people had achieved mightily in their colonizing enterprises in Britain and in Normandy, but the consequence was political disaster at home. The greater part of Denmark, including Hedeby, passed under Swedish lordship. Revival came from a new dynasty, based on Jelling in South Jutland, the kin of Gorm the Old and his wife Thyri who flourished about 940. Harold, their son, raised a memorial stone to them at Jelling some time after 965 on which he was described in runes as 'Harold, who won all Denmark and Norway and made the Danes Christian'. The stone itself is an artistic creation of great merit with splendid interlacing and carving and the figure of Christ crucified in a dominant position. Harold's conquest of Norway proved ephemeral, but his baptism in 965, his active fostering of Christianity, and his administrative gifts helped to make Denmark an effective kingdom.

Harold's own reign ended in personal disaster. His son, Sweyn Forkbeard, turned against him, and the old king, after a reign of some forty years, was wounded and died after a short exile in Slav territory. His body was brought back to Denmark and buried at Roskilde. His son and successor, Sweyn, and more so his grandson, Cnut the Great (King of England 1016–35) continued the dynastic success. Sweyn ruled Denmark for nearly thirty years, and was heavily involved in the conquest of England, dying at Gainsborough on 3 February 1014, shortly after his recognition as king of the English. The best proof archaeologically of the energy and resources of the dynasty is given by the great fortresses now generally dated to the later years of Harold Bluetooth's reign. Sites at Trelleborg near Slagelse in west Zealand, Aggersborg on the Limfjord in north Jutland, Fyrkat near Hobro in east Jutland have been well described: a comparable site at Nonnebakken at Odense in Funen was built over before exact archaeological investigation was possible. They share a common plan, use a common system of mensuration, and were constructed for a common purpose. Aggersborg is the biggest, containing within a circular rampart of 240 metres internal diameter no fewer than 48 identical long wooden houses, each 33 metres in length. At Trelleborg the interior diameter of the rampart is 136 metres and at Fyrkat and Nonnebakken 120 metres. There were 16 identical houses about 30 metres in length at Trelleborg, with a further 15 in the outer defence work, and 16 identical houses (slightly shorter than the main Trelleborg group) at Fyrkat. It has been estimated that the four camps alone could together have housed 4,000 men if they were indeed primarily 'barrácks', but archaeological evidence now suggests that they were fortified settlements of considerable social complexity, including smithies, metal workshops and storehouses with women, children, and craftsmen housed alongside military groups. A puzzling feature is that they seem to have been abandoned after a relatively short active life. Only the king had the resources to build and preserve such defensive works. The fortresses were well placed to control land communications and played a vital part at a critical time in ensuring the maintenance of royal authority in Denmark even when the king was busy elsewhere overseas in English or Norwegian enterprises.

Sweyn died on English campaign in 1014, but Danish ambitions were brought to fruition by his second son Cnut, finally recognized as sole king in England after the death of Edmund Ironside in November 1016. Denmark itself passed to the eldest son, Harold, who died childless in 1019. Cnut thereupon succeeded also to the Danish throne. Much of the later 1020s were occupied with Norwegian affairs and after the death of the Norwegian prince Olaf Haroldsson (St Olaf) in 1030 Cnut seemed effective master of Denmark, Norway, and England. His international reputation was already high. He had been present as an honoured and exalted guest at the imperial coronation of Conrad II in 1027 and remained on good terms with the Empire. But at this moment in the creation of enduring political units the time was not ripe for the permanent establishment of a North Sea empire. Cnut died a relatively young man in 1035, and problems of dynastic succession confirmed a natural split along rudimentary national lines. St Olaf, more popular after death than in life with the Norwegians, had left a son, Magnus, who was acclaimed king of Norway in 1035. Cnut's son Harold Harefoot succeeded to England while his other son Harthacnut became king in Denmark. From the tangled fraternal squabbles of 1036–40 Harthacnut emerged as Harold Harefoot's successor in England but then lost control in Denmark to the Norwegian powers. Harthacnut himself died in 1042 to be succeeded in England by a representative of the ancient West Saxon dynasty in the person of his half-brother, Edward the Confessor. The situation in Denmark itself remained intricate and difficult, and further complicated by the return in the mid-1040s to Northern politics of the charismatic figure of Harold Hardrada, St Olaf's half-brother, with great wealth from his service as captain of the Varangian Guard at Constantinople. The hopes of the Jelling dynasty were kept alive by the skilful and effective nephew of Cnut, Sweyn Estrithsson, the son of Cnut's sister. In 1047 King Magnus of Norway was killed in an accident. For the succeeding seventeen years, a period of relative peace in English affairs under Edward the Confessor, the rivalries of the formidable Harold Hardrada and Sweyn were the dominant features of northern politics. Their rivalries merged into the great crisis that led to the Norman Conquest of England. Hardrada himself was killed at Stamford Bridge in September 1066. Sweyn continued to govern Denmark in his astute and capable fashion until his death in 1074. Intervention in English affairs brought material profit but no permanent gain in 1070 and 1071, though his heirs continued to harbour English ambitions until the assassination of St Cnut in 1086. Sweyn Estrithsson's outstanding contribution, however, lay not so much on the international scene as in his native Danish hearths. By the time of his death Denmark bore the stamp of a permanent Christian kingdom and the Viking days were virtually at an end.

Norway was more backward economically than Denmark and had more difficulties in achieving political shape. Communications overland were exceedingly difficult and there was – and long remained – a tendency for the three principal regions of Norway, the Trondelag, the western fjords, and the Vik (the area of the Oslo fjord), to develop their own independent characteristics, sometimes in conjunction with Danish or Swedish political support. The kings of the first Viking Age had established a firm tradition of Norwegian monarchy and a prince who aspired to wide authority was expected to have or to claim the blood of the Ynglings, preferably direct descent from the prolific Harold Fairhair who died at a great age in or after 931. In the direct line Harold was succeeded by his son Eric Bloodaxe and then much more effectively – with Eric diverted to Viking and English adventures – by another of his sons, Haakon, foster-son of King Athelstan of England. Drawing heavily from his English upbringing and experience Haakon proved himself worthy to rank among the select group of tenth-century rulers who were helping constructively to shape the permanent structure of the European polity. He had drawn up for him and his people codes of laws which were later elaborated into the laws of the Gulathing and

Frostathing. He was responsible for exacting a form of military service based on the land, probably a modified form of the English *fyrd*. In religious matters, although a Christian himself, he did not attempt to convert the still heathen Norwegian peasantry. He died under attack from the Danish king, Harold Bluetooth, in 960, and was succeeded by Harold Greycloak, Haakon's nephew and the son of Eric Bloodaxe. Harold Greycloak, together with his brothers, had spent much of his early life in England and it is undoubtedly true that English religious and political influence had great impact on Norwegian affairs during this period. The impact was not altogether favourable. England itself under Edgar the Peaceful was reaching its height of development. Monarchical institutions were well advanced. The Church under the leadership of St Dunstan and the patronage of King Edgar was strong. The Benedictine revival was well under way and the relationship between king and Church symbolized in the impressive ceremony of royal coronation at Bath in 973. By that time Harold Greycloak was dead, killed in battle against the Danes at Limfjord. He left an unenviable reputation for harshness, mostly apparently because of his precocious attempts to suppress heathen practices. It may well be that the English wine of monarchy and Christianity was too heady for Norway at this stage: the German brew proved much more acceptable in the Danish kingdom.

The last thirty years of the tenth century were an unhappy time in Norwegian political life, heathen, weak, and divided in the face of Danish strength. In 995 Olaf Tryggvasson, a royal prince and one of the most colourful figures of the Viking Age, returned from a successful Viking raid on England, immensely wealthy and a zealous new convert to Christianity. He established himself in the north, in the Trondelag, and attempted to assert his kingship over all Norway. In England he had worked closely with the Danish king Sweyn Forkbeard, but now Sweyn proved too powerful and too adroit for him. Olaf died gallantly but in failure at the naval battle of Svöld in 1000, and Sweyn continued in essential command of Norwegian affairs. The conquest of England, 1013–16, by a curious quirk of fate brought Norway nearer realization of independence. Sweyn died on campaign and his sons Harold and Cnut were both fully occupied in Danish and English affairs for some critical years. A young Norwegian prince, Olaf Haroldsson, representative of a south Norwegian branch of the Ynglings, contended for the throne, defeated the Danish regent in a naval battle, and set himself up as king of Norway, 1016–26. He was a zealous Christian, a harsh reformer, who aroused hostility among the conservative Norwegians. When Cnut had time enough he had little difficulty in overthrowing Olaf and Olaf's final attempt to regain his throne was defeated by the Norwegians themselves at the battle of Stiklestad in the Trondelag. His contribution to Norwegian unity proved, as we said above, greater in death than in life. Men forgot his harsh pro-selytizing, his recruitment of Swedes and other non-Norwegian followers to further his ends, his taxes and his unpopularity. A cult quickly grew up around him. His epic and gallant death in a land battle (and all major political battles in recorded Norwegian history to this point had been sea battles) caused proliferation of legend. These legends, such was the temper of the time, became associated with miraculous cures from sickness, much of the apparatus that was needed to create a popular saint. The Church was quick to act when political circumstances were favourable and Olaf Haroldsson, known as Olaf the Stout, became St Olaf *perpetuus rex Norvegiae.*

Indeed it would be wrong to ignore the very real sentiments of national Norwegian feeling that were now apparent. After the death of Cnut in 1035 St Olaf's son, Magnus, was universally recognized as king in Norway. Such were the precarious circumstances of political life in the North that for a period in the 1040s he even found himself ruling the Danes as well. Under the astute Sweyn Estrithsson (1047–74) the Danes preserved their integrity and independence, but the Norwegians were now for a full generation the dominant political power in the North. Personal credit for this must go in part to Magnus, who left a good reputation as a legislator, and to the forceful Harold Hardrada who succeeded him on the Norwegian throne in 1047. These two rulers, of vastly different temperament and gifts, moulded the identity of historic Norway in the eleventh century. Under them and under Harold's son, Olaf Kyrre, the Peaceful (1066–93), the conversion to Christianity was completed and Norway accepted the pattern of traditional Western Christian monarchy. Harold Hardrada himself epitomizes the changes that had come over the Northern scene in the two Viking centuries. A survivor of Stiklestad where he had fought as a 15-year-old boy by the side of his half-brother, King Olaf, he returned home wealthy and well renowned from service in the Varangian Guard in 1045 to share the throne with his nephew, Magnus. Much of the energy of his full maturity went into schemes of Danish conquest at the expense of the often defeated but ever resilient Sweyn Estrithsson, and he died in his early fifties at the battle of Stamford Bridge, the oldest and most famous of his day of the contenders for the throne of England in 1066. His career, his name (hard-counsel), and his temperament bear many of the marks of the true Viking. But the contrast with the early Viking chiefs is also heavily marked. Harold Hardrada was a leader of national armies, a settled territorial king with ambitions to recreate the empire of Cnut, not a mere leader of Viking bands out for loot. Byzantine wealth and the profits of taxation lay more easily in his treasure chests than gold and silver from despoiled monasteries. He was a successor to King Olaf, a Christian king in his own strange Northern way. For Norway also the Viking Age was drifting towards its Christian end.

The mainland Norwegian story was complicated by the success of her colonizing ventures in the northen islands, the Faroes, Iceland and Greenland. Iceland is far and away the best recorded of all the settlements. The outstanding Icelandic historian of the twelfth century, Ari the Learned, left a brief account, and the *Landnamabok* (or 'Book of Settlements') left a detailed description of the 400 or so chief settlers, 35 of whom had travelled in their own ships. Most were Norwegians from the western fjords or the Islands (it is said that Harold Fairhair, anxious in his days of so-called tyranny for the health of his beloved west and southwest imposed a tax on emigrants to Iceland) and there was also a Celtic element (strong from the Hebrides) which some place as high as 15 per cent. By 930, when the population of Iceland consisted of at least 3,000–4,000 families, regular emigration came to an end, but contact remained a constant and important feature of tenth- and eleventh-century Norwegian life. The settlement flourished and at the end of the tenth century accepted Christianity, largely because of the enterprise and courage of Icelandic supporters of Olaf Tryggvasson. The decision to accept the new faith was carefully debated, and in AD 1000 (possibly 999) it was agreed by law that all should become Christian and be baptized. Some ancient customs, the exposure of children and the eating of horseflesh, were retained, and initially sacrifice in secret to the old gods was permitted. The reaction provoked by the excessive zeal of a Harold Greycloak or Olaf Haroldsson in Norway was avoided and Iceland became a Christian community. Its first native bishop was consecrated by Adalbert of Bremen in 1056. Greenland had been settled from Iceland under the leadership of Eric the Red, and the Greenlanders accepted the Christian faith at the same time as the Icelanders. If their expeditions further west to Vinland and the

American continent had achieved permanent success no doubt there, too, Christian churches would have been built early in the eleventh century. In this respect the outposts anticipated the homeland. The heavy hand of Olaf Tryggvasson proved oddly more effective at a discreet distance.

The history of Sweden from the middle of the tenth century to the end of the eleventh is obscure by the side of her western neighbours. Modern scholarship has emphasized that the very use of the terms 'Sweden' and the 'Swedes' can be misleading, disguising the complexities of the making of the medieval kingdom as the two major peoples, the Swedes and the Geats (*Gautar*) of the south were brought together. But Eastern Scandinavian interest in the expansion along the Russian waterway routes continued; and merchants, sailors and soldiers found an outlet for their energies in opening up routes along the Volga into Central Asia and then later and more permanently along the Dnieper towards Constantinople. In the course of the tenth century the fortified settlements along the waterways civilization of Russia from Novgorod to Kiev became more Slav than Scandinavian, but Swedish enterprise and skill in navigation and trading still had a powerful influence on the development of early Russian communities. The route to Constantinople remained open for hardy traders and fighting men. It would be utterly misleading and inaccurate, however to suggest that Swedish interests lay exclusively to the east. For much of the early tenth century, during a period of Danish weakness, they had threatened to build up a kingdom, based on the trading wealth of Birka and of Hedeby in Schleswig that would incorporate a large part of southern Denmark together with Scania and the heartlands of the Uppsala kingdom into one political unit. There is even evidence of some 'Swedish' settlement to be found in the place-name structure of Zealand itself. Such moves were precocious and impermanent and did not survive the reassertion of Danish strength under Harold Bluetooth. The Swedes remained powerful on the waterways of the eastern Baltic. They controlled most of the islands, particularly Gotland where the settlement at Visby became an important element in the trading life of Scandinavia. The large number of English silver coins of the reign of Ethelred that have been discovered in Gotland testify to the importance of the site and also to the part played by Eastern Scandinavians in Western affairs both directly and indirectly: they took their fair share of Danegeld. In Gotland itself, it has been pointed out that almost all coins found pre-dating 950 are Kufic and that the second half of the tenth century is when the German and English coins appear in force. In the hoards deposited between 990 and 1020 over 40 per cent of the coins were German and 10 per cent English but in the following thirty years 56 per cent were German, 30 per cent English and Kufic contribution had dropped to a mere 5 per cent. Memorial stones with runic inscriptions as well as the tangible evidence of coin hoards tell of their success in the later phases of Viking endeavour during the first half of the eleventh century. England is mentioned directly on no fewer than twenty-five rune stones, none earlier than *c.*AD 1000. We hear of a Viking named Ulf who received tribute three times in England, once from Toste (who may have been the leader of the Swedish contingent), once from Thorkell and once from Cnut himself. Others are said to have received tribute in England, some more than once. Their part in the Western enterprises of the Viking world was indeed far from negligible. They did not provide the leadership, and there may be straightforward technical reasons for this. On the whole, their skills lay in the calmer waters of the Baltic and the Russian rivers. The special skills that went to make the sea-captains of the Atlantic were not theirs. On the other hand there were many Swedes among the ships' crews and more among the settlers in Norway, England, and Iceland than is often believed. Sweden, too, provided a ready home for exiles. Both in history and in saga it is common to find men who later contended successfully for Western thrones spending some years in exile among the Swedes. From time to time the Swedish political powers themselves intervened actively. The victory at sea in the battle of Svöld which resulted in 1000 in the death of Olaf Tryggvasson was a victory for the Swede, Olaf Skotkonung, the first known Christian king of Sweden. Olaf's son, Önund Jacob, rallied to support St Olaf of Norway in 1026 only to meet defeat at the hands of Cnut the Great. By and large, however the Swedish kingdom seems something of a backwater throughout the period.

This impression is heightened when we look at the religious scene. There is an interesting parallel with the Norwegian situation where the colonies overseas accepted Christianity more decisively than the homeland. Strong Christian missionary efforts in the east led to the baptism of Vladimir, Grand Duke of Kiev, in 987, who – an early parallel to St Olaf of Norway – was recognized as a saint soon after his death in 1015. The Swedish kings accepted Christianity in the early eleventh century, but paganism was very strong, particularly around Uppsala. Even as late as the pontificate of Gregory VII in the 1070s a pagan temple still existed in use at Uppsala. The comparative weakness of the Swedish kingship is directly connected with the reluctance of the Swedish community to accept the new faith.

The contrast between Scandinavian history in the first and second Viking centuries is remarkable and significant. For the period that runs up to the mid-tenth century there is a mobility and uncertainty about Scandinavian affairs that is a true product of an age of migration. From the mid-tenth century there is still much mobility and uncertainty, but the context is more cut and dried, more political. The main historical themes, as far as the homeland is concerned, deal with the consolidation of the monarchies and the acceptance of Christianity. Denmark is the earliest to be thoroughly Christianized. English missionaries played their part, but the main impetus was German, continental and indeed after 962 imperial. The north German sees were the active institutional agents, notably the see of Hamburg/Bremen. Norway was more slow-moving and cautious in its acceptance of Christianity. In the early stages English influence was paramount. Iceland was a special case. When organization was needed – and Iceland in these respects as in all others retained its independence and peculiarities – it turned to Germany rather than England; but political accident, notably the great prestige of Hamburg/Bremen under Adalbert in the mid-eleventh century had much to do with this. Sweden was the last of the Scandinavian communities fully to accept Christianity. The strength of the ancient shrines at Uppsala reinforced its native conservatism, but there were also deep social reasons for the slowness of pace. Political life in Denmark and in Norway was more mobile and hectic than in Sweden. The search for a monarchical solution to an overriding problem of law and authority prompted an acceptance of the traditional Western European answer. It is of amusing symbolic note that St Olaf's son, Magnus, who did so much to set the Norwegian monarchy on the right path, took his name from the second element of Charlemagne's name, *Carolus Magnus*. Denmark, Norway, and finally Sweden were brought squarely within the comity of Western monarchies.

By contrast the earlier Viking period seems much more primitive, epic and uncertain. Migration from 800 to 950 must have threatened at times to drain off not only the surplus but the heart and kernel of the native communities just as the movements of the fourth and fifth centuries AD had left large tracts of potentially fertile land deserted. These threats were never realized, and the Scandinavian homelands themselves were ultimately (or so it seemed) strengthened by the colonizing movements overseas. European conditions account in part for this. Feudal institutions, to the growth of which the stimulus of Viking attack in no small measure contributed, slowly brought peace and discipline to the Western world. The revival of the German monarchy and the establishment of the Ottonian empire after 962 gave stability to the Germans, the north Italians, and the inhabitants of the old Middle Kingdom. Scandinavian traders, backed by the guarantee of good standing of Christian monarchs, were welcomed in imperial lands. Greater profit could now be made at infinitely less risk by peaceful traders than by violent looters. The lessons of the Viking Age had been slowly but thoroughly learned in the homelands. Skill at exacting taxes and maintaining permanent armies in communities that were predominantly aggressive had been acquired, notably from English sources. The first Christian Swedish king had the by-name 'Skotkunung', that is to say an exactor of *scot* or *taxes*. Yet one must not paint the picture in too peaceful sedate a style. There were still murderous Vikings on the loose in the Western world late in the eleventh century. The impact of Scandinavian moves onto Britain 954–1087 was often as disastrous as in the earlier migration age. It mattered little to the dispossessed thegn or evicted *ceorl* that he suffered through the actions of national armies rather than murderous migrants. We shall now turn in the next chapter to a consideration of the extent and nature of this impact.

Map 1 Scandinavia in the Viking Age

5

The course of the Scandinavian invasions in Britain and Ireland, c.954–c.1100

England

The nature of the invasions in this period was complex, partly because of the existence of already deep rooted Scandinavian settlements in the British Isles, and partly because of interaction among the various movements and the indigenous peoples. One characteristic is outstanding. We deal now much more than in the earlier period with armies and navies nationally organized with less of an obvious urge for settlement and virtually none of the characteristics of a migration. Wealth, sheer loot, and then political power were the objectives. Chronologically there were three clearcut subperiods. The first generation up to 980 was a time of relative peace. The second up to 1016 was a time of Scandinavian initiative and ultimate domination. The succeeding period experienced a time of extraordinary Danish success followed by recession and then disappearance of Scandinavian pressure.

England demands pride of place in discussion because the maximum Scandinavian efforts in these islands were made successfully in the English direction. Under King Edgar (959–75) the West Saxon monarchy had finally been transformed into a monarchy of all England. Church and state were closely knit together. Full recognition was given to the legal customs of the Danelaw, but the Danish population settled in England were Christian and acknowledged the Christian king, Edgar, as their overlord. After Edgar's death in 975 dynastic weakness revealed flaws in the polity. Edward, his elder son, was murdered at Corfe Castle in circumstances that seemed to incriminate his own stepmother. Her own son, Ethelred, succeeded his half-brother, to rule for the best part of forty years over a kingdom fated to be disrupted and finally conquered by Scandinavian armies. The contemporary Chronicler, the principal narrative source for the reign, clearly loathed Ethelred, attributing English disaster to perfidy and incompetence, starting in the royal person and spreading through the polity. *Ethel-ræd*, the noble counsel, became *Un-ræd*, the no-counsel! England's collapse was a moral collapse, caused negatively by wavering loyalties and positively in church and state by great treachery.

Record of renewed raiding began in 980, and brutal attacks were made widely, against Southampton, the Isle of Thanet, Cheshire, and the southwest. London was looted. A major crisis in 991 was resolved by the battle of Maldon at which the English were defeated in spite of their heroic resistance. Negotiations led to the payment for the first time of Danegeld, the germ of the idea for which was attributed to the archbishop, Sigeric. The English learned the hard way the basic lesson that 'once you have paid them the Danegeld you never get rid of the Dane'. In 994 Olaf Tryggvasson of Norway (who had been prominent in the 991 raids) returned, accompanied by no less a figure than King Sweyn Forkbeard of Denmark with a huge fleet. They won an immense geld for themselves though there were gleams of hope. London beat them off, and in the winter of 994–5 Olaf was converted to Christianity with King Ethelred acting as his sponsor. Olaf promised not to come back in hostility, and kept that promise. But from 997, after a very short lull, attacks were continuous. In vivid prose the Anglon-Saxon Chronicle painted a dismal picture of useless activity and treachery. English forces were constantly wrong-footed. Their men or ships were in the one quarter when the Scandinavians were in the other. No part of England was free from ravaging. The Danes were able in their pride to ride within sight of the walls of Winchester unharmed. Graphic accounts were given of tales of treachery on both sides: a massacre of Danes of St Brice's Day, 1002, in which Sweyn's sister was said to have perished; the martyrdom of Archbishop Ælfheah at Canterbury in 1012. Modern scholars have pointed out that all the blame should not be laid on Ethelred's shoulders, and indeed all was not gloom. In the financial and legal fields solid advance was made. England enjoyed the benefit of a stable and strictly regulated coinage. The courts of the shires, hundreds and wapentakes were well organized, and the royal role as the source of law-codes applicable to the whole community heavily emphasized. This was a great age of vernacular scholarship with Ælfric and Wulfstan the outstanding scholars. Benedictine monasticism flourished in spite of the barbarian raids. But the general suffering over a period of some twenty years was great. The Danes seemed for the most part to have the best of both worlds: much loot, come by at no great cost, and fat tribute efficiently collected for them by the wealthy territorial government of King Ethelred.

By 1014 England was ready to accept the Danish Sweyn as their own king, and Ethelred went into exile in Normandy. Sweyn's untimely death in February gave the old dynasty a further chance. Ethelred returned, and his able son and successor, Edmund Ironside, initially achieved a balance of power with Sweyn's son, Cnut. Edmund himself, however, died young, and the Danish Cnut was universally recognized as king of the English in late 1016.

Cnut's victory was followed by a Danish interlude in English political history (1016–42) during which descendants of Gorm the Old occupied the English throne. Cnut was one of the great men of the period, and proved to be a powerful agent in bringing the Viking Age to an end. He stressed continuity with the settled English past. He ordered Emma, Ethelred's widow, to be brought from Normandy, and married her. Right through to her death in 1052, this Norman princess, the Lady of Winchester, wife to two kings of England, mother to two more, exercised great political influence. Cnut continued to use some of Ethelred's close advisers, especially Wulfstan, archbishop of York, who drafted the king's authoritative statements of Anglo-Saxon law. He showed all the fervour of the convert in upholding Christianity and Christian kingship. England became his favoured home, even after he succeeded to the Danish throne in 1019. The solemn translation of the relics of the martyred archbishop, Ælfheah, from London to Canterbury in June, 1023, in the presence of King Cnut, Queen Emma and their young son Harthacnut symbolizes the metamorphosis of this young, barbaric prince who had mutilated his hostages in 1014, into a Christian king.

Cnut continued also to be active and ultimately successful in northern politics, using English resources to that end. He was largely responsible for the defeat and death of Olaf Haroldson (St Olaf) in 1030, and governed Norway through regents with intermittent success. At the height of his power he could make good the boast implicit in his title that he was king of all England, and of

Denmark, and of the Norwegians, and part of the Swedes. The encomiast of his wife, Emma, described him as emperor of five kingdoms. On the international scale he visited and was spendidly received by both the pope and the emperor, and negotiated trade agreements to the advantage of England. He died at Shaftesbury on 12 November 1035, under forty years of age, and was buried at Winchester. He had given England nearly twenty years of peace and prosperity.

The succession was uncertain, and fear of a return to the turbulence of Ethelred's day led to a series of uneasy compromises between parties formed around Cnut's two sons, Harthacnut and Harold, and ultimately to the restoration of the old dynasty in the person of Edward the Confessor, recalled from his Norman exile in 1041 by Harthacnut, his own younger half-brother. The solidity of the Old English administration, the power of the new earldoms created by Cnut, and the presence of a well paid navy helped to preserve stability though there is evidence, too, of violence near the surface in, for example, the murder of prince Alfred, Edward's brother, in 1036 by Harold Harefoot's orders, and the harshness of Harthacnut's tax collectors.

Edward succeeded Harthacnut in June, 1041, and proved able by skill and luck to keep his kingdom in substantial peace right through to the time of his death in the first week of 1066. A deep desire to keep the kingdom free from Viking ravaging and from civil war contributed to his success. So did the changes that were coming over the Northern world itself. Both Denmark and Norway were heavily concerned for much of his reign with their own internal affairs, part of the painful process of growth to nationhood. In making his successful bid for the English throne Harthacnut had lost control of Danish affairs. The Norwegian prince, Magnus the Good, son of St Olaf, took his opportunity, and, already secure in Norway, extended his authority over Denmark also for most of the 1040s until his death in the autumn of 1047. By that date two master figures had emerged from the tangle of Dano-Norwegian politics and dynastic history, Harold Hardrada, King of Norway (1047–66) and Sweyn Estrithsson, King of Denmark (1047–74). Their rivalry heralded a fitting domestic conclusion to the Viking story in the North and relieved much of the pressure on England. Edward with the sometimes uncertain but always vigorous help of Earl Godwin, of Harold, son of Godwin, and others of that formidable kin, was able to safeguard his borders, and impose internal peace, even to the point where he paid off a substantial portion of his standing fleet in 1050. Viking raids still continued. In 1058 a major attack took place, led by Magnus, son of Harold Hardrada, but this was exceptional. By and large the raids were no more than minor, spasmodic and local, undertaken from the western Isles, the Isle of Man, and Ireland.

Both of the northern kings retained an interest in the English succession, Harold Hardrada possibly from promises said to have been made to his nephew, Magnus the Good, Sweyn more tangibly from his right of blood as nephew of King Cnut. Harold, with his by-name of 'hard-counsel', had many of the traditional attributes of a Viking chief. He was a survivor of the battle of Stiklestad in 1030 at which his half-brother, St Olaf, had met his death. He had won fortune for himself in the Varangian Guard at Constantinople, and remained a captain of fighting men up to the end at Stamford Bridge. His major contribution to Norwegian history, however, is more prosaic. In nearly twenty years of vigorous rule and campaigning, mostly against the Danes, he consolidated the political structure of Norway, confirming the permanent conjunction of the Oslo fjord with Bergen and Nidaros. The chance for English adventure came in 1065–6, the last year of the Confessor's reign and that of his successor, Harold II of England, Harold, son of Godwin. The sheer size of the Norwegian intervention in September 1066 is proof that we deal with something more than a Viking raid. Reinforced by the Earl of Orkney and by Harold's disaffected brother, Tostig, Hardrada's fleet is said to have consisted of some 300 ships, manned by at least 9,000 men. After initial success he was defeated at Stamford Bridge not far from York, and his defeat was truly overwhelming: a couple of dozen ships were enough to take the survivors back to the North. Harold's son, later known as Olaf Kyrre, the peaceable, was among the survivors. In the following century there were occasional Norwegian raids, operating for the most part along the western shores from bases in the northern and western isles. The Viking Age, as far as the Norwegians were concerned, ended with the death of Harold Hardrada at Stamford Bridge on 25 September 1066.

English victory at Stamford Bridge was followed within three weeks by devastating defeat at the hands of William of Normandy at Hastings on Saturday, 14 October 1066. There remains the Danish side of things to consider. Sweyn Estrithsson seems in 1066 to have given some diplomatic support to William. His main delight would surely have been to see the immense fleet prepared by Harold Hardrada moved west over sea to England rather than south against Denmark. When William's settlement of England ran into its earliest and greatest crisis, 1069–71, Sweyn judged the time ripe for intervention but allowed himself to be bought off, so losing the last serious opportunity of an enduring Anglo-Danish kingdom. One further effort was made under Cnut, Sweyn's son and successor, in 1083, threatening enough to prompt William to recruit heavily in France, but the murder of the Danish king ended the threat. Contact between Denmark and England remained significant economically and socially. Privileges in London and on the eastern seaboard were granted to Danish merchants. But the Norman duke-kings brought England securely into the Gallic Romanic orbit. To raid England ceased to be profitable, and from Denmark as from Norway the danger of political conquest disappeared. The Normans may have plundered their subjects: they certainly protected them from others. In that sense the Norman Conquest provided a clear terminal point to the Viking Age for the English realm.

Wales

The middle of the tenth century marks the end of an important phase in Welsh political history, and the beginning of a new chapter in its contacts with the Scandinavians. Wales had weathered the first Viking onslaughts exceedingly well. Alone of the principal political units of Britain it had avoided yielding tracts of territory to Scandinavian adventures. Credit for this must go largely to the leadership first of Rhodri Mawr (844–78) and then of Hywel Dda (c.926–50). Rhodri had been killed by the English but his successors, especially his grandson, Hywel, worked closely with their fellow-Christian English against the heathen Danes. There was a positive lull in Scandinavian activity in Wales in the second quarter of the tenth century, possibly associated with indications of Danish presence in Brittany between 920 and 940. Hywel's death in 950, however, was followed by a long period of civil dissension and raids from oversea, mostly by Scandinavian settlers in easy distance from Welsh shores, men from Dublin and other Irish ports, men from the Isle of Man and the Hebrides. There was no systematic purpose behind the attacks of the type only too obvious in Ethelred's England, at most perhaps an attempt to set up safe bases for ships in Pembrokeshire and Anglesey. Loot, especially silver and treasures from monasteries of easy access, was the prime aim. St David's was sacked no fewer than three times in the last twenty years of the century, and Llandbadarn Fawr, St Dogmaels, Llanilltud and Llancarfan all suffered. The ancient kingdom of Gwynedd was also ravaged, particularly Anglesey, the target for at least three full-scale expeditions directed from the Isle of Man. Welsh princes, myopically concerned with their own internecine conflicts, made some use of Scandinavian seamen as mercenaries. Maredudd ab Owain (986–99), a powerful ruler in Deheubarth, who had himself used such mercenaries, was compelled to pay a penny a head to redeem Welsh prisoners at the height of the Norse attacks.

Wales played little part in the crises that racked England during the reign of Ethelred, a contrast to its role in the Alfredian period. Sea communications remained strong with Ireland, and an outstanding feature of the eleventh century was the growth of a recognizable Irish Sea political circle in which the old identities of Scandinavian and Celt became blurred. Exiles from Ireland found refuge in Wales, and exiles from Wales found refuge in Ireland. Gruffydd ap Cynan, the ruler of Gwynedd from 1075 (with interruptions) to his death in 1137, was said to have been born in exile in Dublin in 1054 or 1055 and brought up in the Scandinavian settlement there. Raids continued late into the eleventh century, increasingly as incidental irritants. Pressure from England was the dominant political issue, successfully resisted by the north Welsh prince of Gwynedd, Gruffydd ap Llewelyn, until he was overwhelmed by Harold Godwinsson in 1063. A Norwegian fleet, led by Magnus, son of Harold Hardrada, had helped Gruffydd in 1058, probably in the course of testing the political temperature in England. The Norman Conquest of England intensified pressure from the new Norman earls of Hereford (to 1076), Shrewsbury, and Chester. The end of the true Viking intervention in Wales came towards the end of the century in relation to the ambition of these earls. Hugh Lupus, earl of Chester, accompanied by Hugh Montgomery, earl of Shrewsbury, made a decisive effort to master north Wales in 1098. The native Welsh princes withdrew to Anglesey, relying on a fleet of Scandinavian-Irish mercenaries for support. The mercenaries proved treacherous, and Gruffydd ap Cynan fled to Ireland. Anglesey was ravaged by the Normans, and the conquest seemed complete, when a Norwegian fleet, commanded by Magnus Barefoot, king of Norway, appeared off Priestholm. In the ensuing battle the earl of Shrewsbury was killed,

reputedly by the Norwegian king himself, and the extreme pre-
cariousness of the Norman hold on Anglesey made evident. No
further systematic attempt to conquer Wales west of Conway was
to be made for many generations. This last intrusion of Scandinavian power into Welsh affairs, an accidental by-product of royal
Norwegian concern to demonstrate authority in the Scottish Isles
and Man, typifies the contact of Scandinavians with Wales: mysterious, incidental, and in the last resort of fringe importance. Contact with Ireland was quite a different story.

Ireland

The middle of the tenth century marked an important stage also
in the history of Ireland. From 920 to 950 serious attempts had
been made to create a joint kingdom of Dublin and York. Olaf
Sihtricson, better known as Olaf Cuaran, twice established himself
as king at York, but in 952 finally gave up his Northumbrian ambitions and resumed his kingship in Dublin. For close on thirty years
he ruled the Scandinavian colony there vigorously. He married an
Irish princess with the result that his sons could draw on loyalties
from both communities. He was converted to Christianity. When,
in 980, his sons were defeated by the Irish high-king at Tara, Olaf
fled the country, dying a simple Christian pilgrim at Iona. He was
succeeded by his son, Gluniarainn, who entered an alliance with the
man who had defeated him, his Irish-kinsman, Mael Sechnaill
(Malachy) even against his fellow Vikings of Waterford who had
temporarily taken over control of Dublin. In 994 Mael Sechnaill
drove the Waterford Vikings out of Dublin, and another of Olaf
Cuaran's son Sihtric of the Silken Beard, succeeded to the kingship.
His fortunes became bound up with the career of one of the giant
figures of early Irish history, Brian Boru. Born in 941, Brian gained
his military reputation in campaigns against the Vikings of Limerick,
and by 984 was overlord of most southern Ireland in an increasingly
uneasy relationship with the high-king Mael Sechnaill whose power
centre lay to the north. Complicated alliances among petty princes
destroyed what balance existed and in 999, after a ferocious battle
Brian captured Dublin. Sihtric came to terms, and so did Mael
Sechnaill who, in 1001–2 yielded his high-kingship to Brian. In 1005
at Armagh in the north Brian was being styled *imperator Scottorum*,
emperor of the Irish.

The decade or so of Brian's high-kingship created legends of unity greater then the reality. Dissensions among the Irish rulers erupted into warfare, culminating in one of the most famous battles of the period, fought at Clontarf on Good Friday, 23 April 1014. The battle was not a straight issue between the Irish and the Vikings. Sihtric of the Silken Beard had enlisted help along the whole of the western Viking world in support of his fortified market at Dublin, from Iceland to Orkney, the Isle of Man and even Normandy; but a strong detachment from the Isle of Man supported Brian Boru. There were Christians and pagans on both sides. Nor was it a clear conflict between centralizing forces represented by Brian, and the forces of localism. The heart of the political matter seems to have been an assertion of strength on the part of the men of Leinster against Brian with the Norsemen active but essentially of secondary importance. The result was chaotic. Brian, his son, and his grandson were all killed in the battle or its aftermath. On the Viking side, Sigurd, earl of Orkney, and Brodir, who had brought twenty ships from the Isle of Man, both perished. Brian in legend was held to have saved Ireland by his victory, but it is hard to say from what. None of the Vikings aspired to his high-kingship. The Scandinavian settlements were too useful to the native Irish to be eradicated, but they were not strong enough to hope to achieve complete political mastery. In the event, the dynastic turbulence that followed Clontarf led to a weakening of the moves towards unity, and the Scandinavian settlements persisted though more confined. Mael Sechnaill was once again recognized as high king. Scandinavian kings continued at Dublin (Sihtric himself surviving into the 1030s) and a heavily Scandinavianized population remained, known in time as Ostmen, to play a vital role in the trade of the western seaboard from Dublin itself and from Waterford, Wexford, Cork, and Limerick. In 1052 a military defeat led to the flight of the Scandinavian king from Dublin, but the old dynasty returned in the early twelfth century. Not until the 1160s were the Scandinavian princelings finally removed as part of the complicated process that brought the Anglo-Normans into Ireland.

Scotland, the Northern Isles, the Western Isles, and Man

No part of Great Britain was more directly affected by the Scandinavian invasions than the elaborate complex of islands that stretches from the tip of Shetland south-west around the coast of Scotland into the Irish Sea, islands that we know as the Shetlands, the Orkneys, the Hebrides, the Sudreys, and Man – or sometimes in simpler but more archaic fashion as the Nordreys and the Sudreys. Many of these islands were early settled by Norwegians. They remained on one of the main Viking routes, subject to raids and settlement sporadically throughout the Viking Age. They were also vastly important staging posts for many enterprises further south, a useful intermediary point for raiding fleets from Scandinavia, convenient places to refit and to recover from the arduous sea passage from Nidaros, the western fjords, or the Vik. In 1066 Orkney played a big part in the events that led up to the battles of Fulford Gate and Stamford Bridge, and it was to Orkney that the young prince Olaf Haroldsson brought the pitiful remnant of the Scandinavian host after the defeat at Stamford Bridge.

The most important and most prosperous of the settlements – with the possible exception of Man – was the settlement in Orkney. The family of Ragnald, jarl of Möre in western Norway, which provided Normandy with its ducal house, was also prominent in Orkney affairs. Ragnald's brother, Sigurd the Great, had acted more or less as Harold Fairhair's regent and had won control of extensive territory in north Scotland in Caithness, Sutherland, and even into Ross-shire and south of the Moray Firth. Ragnald's youngest son, Turf-Einar, did not enjoy the same extensive authority as his uncle Sigurd, but later poetic and part legendary accounts attributed to him not only the credit for introducing the skills of the peat-burner to the islanders but also the credit for setting up the earl's authority and power on a more territorial basis. He was reputed to have paid a substantial fine on behalf of the islanders (60 marks of gold) to the Norwegian king in return for the surrender on the part of the free farmers of their odal rights to him. The story has the smack of the later twelfth- or thirteenth-century feudal world to it, but there may be some truth in the idea that the family of Ragnald was trying to consolidate its position in Orkney during the early part of the tenth century. The middle years of the tenth century saw no dramatic watershed in events of the type we have seen in Scandinavian affairs elsewhere in Britain. As far as there is one single dominant thread to the political story it concerns the fortunes of the house of Ragnald, its marriage alliances, its quarrels with other powers (including fellow-Vikings such as the dynasty of Limerick Vikings established in Man) and its relationship – which generally followed the theme of nominal dependence and virtual independence – with the Norwegian crown. Caithness was brought back into the Orkney orbit by a marriage agreement made by one of Turf-Einar's sons and a princess of the mainland. Further dynastic marriages with Irish chieftains brought extra influence and security in the Western Isles. The son of one of these marriages, Sigurd the Stout, brought fresh prestige to the dynasty at the end of the tenth and the beginning of the eleventh century. In 995 Sigurd suffered a conversion to Christianity as sudden and dramatic if not as deep and long-lasting as any in recorded history. We are told that the stormy, newly converted Olaf Tryggvasson came across him suddenly and by chance in the bay of Osmondwall (Kirk Hope) and gave him the straight choice of death and destruction or conversion. The dramatic nature of this account, taken from the Orkneyinga Saga, must not obscure the fact that many men in the Northern Isles were Christians long before 995. Sigurd accepted conversion, built up a powerful hold on Caithness and the Southern Isles, placed a subordinate earl in charge of Man, and married as his second wife a daughter of Malcolm II of Scotland (1005–34). He was the linchpin of the Viking federation hastily summoned to the aid of the Dublin Vikings in 1014 and his death at the resulting battle of Clontarf was as momentous in Northern history as the death of Brian Boru himself. He was succeeded by his son, Thorfinn later known as 'the Mighty', the most colourful of the Orkney earls (1014–64). Thorfinn's inheritance was turbulent. For the first twenty years of his active political life up to the death of his grandfather, Malcolm of Scotland, he was engaged in family feuding with his half-brothers and power-sharing in the islands (under the watchful eye in the 1020s of Olaf Haraldsson, St Olaf of Norway). Malcolm's death was followed by an unsuccessful attempt on the part of his successor, Duncan I (1034–40) to recover Caithness, an attempt which left Thorfinn temporarily confirmed in the leadership of all the Northern Vikings. Norwegian interference at the time of Magnus Olafsson forced further power-sharing in the Orkneys, this time with Ragnald, the son of Thorfinn's half-brother, Brusi. The arrangement worked well until the mid-1040s when a violent quarrel sprang up that ended with the slaying of Ragnald as he fled from his blazing Orkney homestead at Christmastide. For the greater part of the reign of Edward the Confessor in England (1042–66) and of Harold Hardrada in Norway (1047–66) Thorfinn consolidated his hold on the northern and western seaways of Britain. He was a Christian and founded the first regular bishop's see in the Northern Isles at Birsay where he was given Christian burial at his death in 1064. He was strong enough and confident enough to journey abroad and record has survived of a visit to Rome, as well as of visits to Denmark and to German imperial lands. He recognised the overlordship of Hardrada, king of Norway, while enjoying almost unfettered rule of Shetland, Orkney and the Hebrides. He also governed the Sudreys and (after 1034) reasserted the rights of the Orkney earls over Man. His relationship with the Scottish kings was predictably complex. At the height of his power Thorfinn was said to have held no fewer than nine Scottish earldoms, including Ross, a part of Moray, and Galloway. It is hard to know how much to make of this. He was certainly effective in the northern mainland and also in Galloway where he liked to reside and which he liked to use as a base for ventures in the Southern Isles and Man. Towards the end of his life the formidable new Scottish king, Malcolm Canmore, Malcolm III (1058–93), asserted his rights over most of mainland Scotland. Thorfinn's achievements were beyond question great, but it would be utterly wrong to consider him as a builder of a permanent empire of the Isles and of Man. His authority depended much on his personal vigour and on his personal presence. His father Sigurd is said to have granted back odal rights to the Orkney landowners and whatever truth there may or may not be in that precise statement it is beyond question that the basic social composition on most of the islands consisted of hardy independent fishermen-farmers, only too ready to turn to Viking enterprise if the leadership were good and the prospects for profit reasonable. Thorfinn's basic achievement was to sharpen for these men their sense of awareness of common kinship with the Norwegian home-land, not to mould them into a permanent independent polity. By the time of his death or very soon after the Isle of Man passed under the control of Vikings from Dublin. Godfred Sihtricson, one of the survivors from Stamford Bridge, is described as a king of Man. He took back with him from Stamford Bridge Godred Crovan, a man whose father was an Icelander, and Godfred after a chequered career in Norway itself won a kingship in Man for himself (1079–95), transmitting rights to his descendants notably to his son Olaf who governed Man from 1113 to 1153. Orkney itself tended to be divided and subdivided amongst the numerous heirs of Thorfinn after 1064 – a ready and natural fate for any island polity – until the Norwegian king Magnus Barefoot intervened in person towards the end of the eleventh century. We have already seen the disastrous impact of his activities on Welsh affairs in 1098. In the Orkneys he removed the quarrelsome earls and put his own son Sigurd in command. Further south he saw to it – probably the main object of his expedition – that the Sudreys and Man paid their tribute to their rightful king, the ruler of Norway. After Sigurd himself became the Norwegian king in 1103, the grandsons of Thorfinn were permitted to resume earlish office in the North. Northern Island history remained turbulent and fluctuating throughout the twelfth and most of the thirteenth century, but we now move out of the true Viking Age. Man and the Western Isles remained under nominal and at times effective Norwegian overlordship until 1266, when after a series of Scottish victories the young king Magnus ceded to Alexander II of Scotland the lordship of the Isle of Man and of all the Sudreys in return for a payment of 4,000 marks (at the rate of 1,000 marks a year) and of 100 marks a year thereafter. Orkney and Shetland were under Scandinavian sovereignty for a further two centuries. The earls became Scottish, and Norway itself became a joint kingdom of Denmark – Norway, ruled by a Danish dynasty. The 100 marks a year payment, agreed on in 1266, was paid only intermittently, and in the 1460s the final attempt at a solution to the problem of the islands was in fact made. In 1468 a marriage contract was arranged between King James III of Scotland and Margaret, a Danish princess, the daughter of King Christian I. The agreement was drawn up formally on 8 September. Christian remitted the annual payment of 100 marks, forgave all the accumulated arrears, and granted 60,000 Rhenish florins as his daughter's dowry, 10,000 to be paid in cash and the other 50,000 promised with the Orkneys held in pledge until the debt was redeemed. Christian could not find even the 10,000 initial payment, and so on 28 May 1469, he pledged Shetland on the same conditions for 8,000 of the promised florins. The islands were pawned not ceded, but political circumstances ensured that the arrangements should become permanent. Shetland came in almost fortuitously: earlier efforts to link it with the Faroes had not proved successful. On the same day that he pawned Shetland King Christian I wrote to the inhabitants of Orkney and Shetland, instructing them to do homage to the Scottish king and to pay their taxes to him until the islands were redeemed. More than half a millennium later they are still doing so: an odd quirk of an end to a brave story of colonization and settlement from the Viking Age.

6

The effects of the Scandinavian invasions on Britain: the problem of settlement

To this point we have been concerned mainly with the general political impact of the Scandinavian invasions on Britain. The time has now come to attempt a deeper evaluation of the effects. Some of these effects are beyond the province of the historian, given our present limitations of admissible evidence. The sheer addition in genetic terms of Scandinavian blood into the human stock peopling these islands must have been considerable. Intermarriage was never discouraged and a recognized place was found in Scandinavian legal systems for sexual unions that fell well short of recognizable Christian marriage. Study of blood groups and methods of evaluation of nigrescence are imperfect disciplines and with each generation that passes hope of establishing regional variations that will help to trace direct Scandinavian influence from the time of the migration grows dimmer and dimmer. And yet historians are right still to think in these human terms. Over large tracts of the British Isles the Scandinavians formed an important recognizable element in the human population. The Middle Ages was fully aware of this, and treated the matter as a commonplace. When Giraldus Cambrensis wished to explain the origins of the peculiar style of part-singing characteristic of Wales and of the lands beyond the Humber and on the borders of Yorkshire, he attributed it directly to the Danes and Norwegians by whom those parts of the island were frequently ruled. It is a pleasant thought that to one shrewd medieval observer characteristics common to the ancestors of the Treorchy Male Voice Choir and the choral societies of Leeds and

Huddersfield were attributable to a common subjection to Scandinavian mastery.

The main source of evidence for adequate discussion of intensity of settlement are relatively prosaic, and all have limitations and imperfections. The existence of distinctive art forms, classified in orderly though at times overlapping chronological sequence help to indicate strong Scandinavian presence in Britain. The Borre and Jellinge styles of the first Viking Age lead into the Mammen, Ringerike and Urnes style of the later tenth and eleventh centuries. Stone crosses and memorial slabs provide the most fruitful, truly monumental, sources, but the interlace, and the main zoomorphic elements in birds and beasts, are to be found also on small metalwork objects and fragments of carved wood. Examples are widespread throughout Scandinavian Britain, in the Vale of Pickering in east Yorkshire, in the north west, and most powerfully in the Isle of Man itself. Current orthodox opinion would attribute native stylistic forms, even the Anglian characteristics of the Middleton sculptures and Irish elements in the Isle of Man, to something of a secondary nature. The vital creative stylistic impulses seem to have been generated in Scandinavian soil, though modifications particularly where a strong native tradition of stone-carving is known to have flourished, at times lead the archaeologist or art historian to talk in the rather awkward terms of 'insular-Jellinge' or 'insular-Ringerike'. The force of the artistic impulse extended well beyond the Danelaw in space and beyond the Norman Conquest in time. One of the finest examples of modified Ringerike occurs in the early eleventh-century tombstone found in St Paul's churchyard, London. The vigorous and imaginative school of stone sculpture centred at Kilpeck in Herefordshire in mid-twelfth century bore the characteristics of developed Urnes style. However intimate the intermingling of Celtic, Anglian and Viking elements, the lesson of the art historian teaches us not to underestimate the direct and enduring influence of Scandinavia on British life.

The principal and strongest body of evidence relating to Scandinavian settlement comes, however, from language sources, among which place-name and personal-name evidence take on a special life of their own, and from evidence drawn from institutional sources. In language matters England is in a separate and distinctive category within the British scene. Anglo-Saxon was a Germanic language, cognate to and in basic structure very similar to Old Norse. An Icelandic author could comment in the thirteenth century that up to the time of William the Bastard the language of England was one and the same as that in Norway and Denmark, and that it was only after his conquest that there was a change of tongue to French – because William was of French extraction. The conventions of writing tend to exaggerate rather than diminish the differences between the two Germanic languages but enough of the similarities shine through in any comparison of similar passages, especially those of scriptural material, in Old English and Old Norse. There was more to it than mere regional dialectical variation, but missionaries, traders and soldiers seem to have experienced little linguistic difficulty in moving from England to the Scandinavian North. This is a point, of course, of marked contrast with the rest of the British Isles. The Celtic tongues, Goidelic or Brythonic, of Ireland, Scotland and Wales, were Indo-European, but remote in structure, sound-change, and vocabulary from the Germanic tongues. Conscious and sustained effort had to be made by Celtic-speakers and Scandinavians alike in order to understand and be understood. There could be no slow folding together of language elements such as occurred in the Danelaw in England. Linguistic evidence therefore demands a different and in some respects a more cautious approach in relation to English problems than in relation to the Celtic world. By 1100 the very nature of the English language itself in the east and north had been profoundly modified to the point where it is not unreasonable to call it Anglo-Scandinavian; and it was from the language pattern of eastern England that the main lines of standard modern English were ultimately to develop.

The whole linguistic situation in England is complicated by the poverty of written record in Old Norse that can be ascribed to the period of invasion and settlement. There is no surviving substantial literary text, and the assumption is that when the Scandinavian settlers were converted to Christianity, the religion of written record, they were also converted linguistically to the use of Latin and of Anglo-Saxon. Archbishop Wulfstan was bishop of Worcester and archbishop of York from 1002 to 1023. He was a conscientious bishop and a voluminous and effective writer and teacher. The Scandinavian element in his vocabulary was distinctly large and gives a quite individual character to many of his homilies as well as to his legal writings. His language is nevertheless unmistakably Anglo-Saxon, and indeed basically the language of Wessex, the accepted *Schriftssprache* of late Anglo-Saxon England. Attempts to prove Anglian peculiarities as opposed to West Saxon have not been successful. If this is true of Wulfstan whose archiepiscopal diocese contained the heavily Scandinavian centre of York and whose king was finally Cnut, how much more true it is of other late Old English writers. There is no fragment of the Gospels, no scriptural text, no liturgical phrase which can be traced to an Old Norse speaker resident in England. The converted Dane worshipped in English – or in Latin. Orm, the son of Gamol, renewed the church of St Gregory in heavily Scandinavianized Kirkdale in Yorkshire in the days of Earl Tostig (1055–65). He recorded his munificence in a still surviving inscription attached to the sundial over the lintel of the south porch and the language used in the inscription was standard Old English with Northumbrian features and only one obvious Scandinavian loanword (*solmerca* (sun-marking) from the Old Norse *solmerki*). When a writ was issued in the middle years of the eleventh century by Gospatric, lord of Allerdale and Dalston, relating to grants of lands and rights in Cumberland, the language used was Old English in spite of the fact that the principal men concerned bore Scandinavian names; indeed the use of the Old Norse term *dreng* in the writ may be taken as evidence that drengs were as firmly naturalized in the social scene of northern England as were earls throughout the length and breadth of the country.

The Scandinavians were not however completely illiterate. There are a number of runic inscriptions in England, many of which for simple natural reasons of weathering have been worn away to the point where they are virtually illegible. Inscriptions on sword-hilts, bone combs, as well as on funerary stones show that Old Norse remained a fully inflected language, subject to the same sound changes and developments in England as back home in the Scandinavian mainland. The phrases inscribed are standard and often not particularly informative: 'Thorfastr made a good comb' (on a bone comb found at Lincoln); 'Ginna and Toki had this stone set up' (on a stone in St Paul's churchyard, London); 'Dolfinn wrote these runes on this stone' (graffito within the cathedral at Carlisle). The custom of fashioning runic inscriptions persisted long and there are occasionally more interesting examples to be found in the twelfth or even the thirteenth century. Towards the end of the eleventh or the beginning of the twelfth century Mael-Lomchon, a Manx Norseman (together with the daughter of Dubh-Gael whom Aðils had to wife) raised a cross in memory of her foster-mother, Mael-Muire, adding a gnomic comment 'it is better to leave a good foster-son than a bad son'.

The most impressive of a whole set of twelfth-century runic inscriptions within the great chambered burial mound at Maeshowe in Orkney records how Crusaders on their way to Jerusalem (probably 1150-1) broke into the mound only to find that the treasure had been removed – through good treasure was still hidden to the north west and 'happy would he be who could find it'! One of the rune-cutters claimed to be the man most skilful in rune-craft west over sea. The skill of carving runes persisted, notably in the ambiance of Man, Ireland and the islands. On the Scandinavian/Irish mainland of north-west England again as late as the mid-twelfth century an inscription was cut in runes on the tympanum of the old church at Pennington in Furness that appears to record that 'Gamal founded [*seti?*] this church; Hubert the mason carved [it?]'. It is reasonable to conclude that the two languages remained in intimate contact in north-west England in the twelfth century.

Old Norse continued therefore to be spoken in Britain well beyond the Viking period. Even after proper discount is made for the conservative nature of those who carve runes, it is clear that British Old Norse was exceedingly tenacious of old forms, to the point indeed where it must have appeared archaic to the rest of the Scandinavian world. Under the powerful influence of early Middle English it became corrupt and anglicized even in the north west, though the strong element of Scandinavian language forms in the great alliterative verse of the north west in the fourteenth century testifies to its tenacity. There appears to have been very little difference between cast and west Scandinavian, between Danish and Norwegian, at the time of the settlement, though words that are unquestionably Danish include *tro* (faith), *lune* (peace) and *bop* (booth).

It is likely that old Norse remained more or less intelligible in the Danelaw at least into the first or second generation after the Norman Conquest and that traders at York (and indeed in London) found little language difficulty until about the mid-twelfth century. Anglo-Saxon and its successor early Middle English triumphed, however, as the current everyday language. Officially, too, at the local level English proved overwhelmingly strong. Communications by sea remained important, and contacts with the Isle of Man, the Irish ports and the Northern and Western Isles, all of which contained a substantial and influential Norse-speaking population well into the twelfth century (and in some instances much later), helped to keep the Norse tongue alive. Traditional literary Anglo-Saxon, affected by the conservatism of a mature written convention, shows (except in the legal field) comparatively little sign of this long linguistic symbiosis. The spoken language, especially in the north and east, was a very different matter. The impact of Old Norse on English vocabulary was deep and widespread. The process of borrowing and of assimilation appears to have been continuous throughout the Viking period and into the twelfth century. Few Norse loanwords, if any, were borrowed from the Continent after about the middle of the tenth century. Borrowings are more intimate, arising from communities dwelling closely together, intermingling and intermarrying, subjects of the same Christian kings, English or Danish or Norman. The vocabulary so acquired enriched English not in an exotic, specialized sense but in a most general sense. Words to denote the most common of actions ('to call' and 'to take') were adopted. Household, everyday words such as 'husband', 'window', 'knife', 'fellow' were absorbed into what must truly be called an Anglo-Scandinavian Germanic language. Even the inner core of the language, pronoun structure and terms connected with the family, were affected. The pronoun structure of Anglo-Saxon had developed along lines that must have led to serious ambiguities in the spoken tongue, notably in relation to the third person plural. Borrowings from Scandinavian sources (though there are some indications notably in the Sherborne Cartulary of indigenous moves in this direction) helped to clarify the situation, and 'she', 'they', 'them', 'their' became part of the basic structure of the language. Other words essential to the grammatical flexibility of the language were also introduced or modified by contact with Old Norse. Modern English 'sister' owes its final form more to Old Norse *syster* than to Old English *sweoster*. Even the word 'to die' is probably derived from the West Norse *deyja*. In more specialized fields, notably those of law and administration, Old Norse influence is heavy ('law', itself, 'outlaw', 'earl' in the new administrative eleventh-century sense in place of Old English *ealdorman*, 'hold', 'husting' to describe the regular weekly court for the settlement of civil business in pre-Conquest London, 'thrall', and a whole mass of precise legal terminology such as *grith* (peace) in its various forms). The language evidence remains the cornerstone of the argument in favour of an interpretation of the Scandinavian invasion and settlement of England that will stress the numbers, influence and permanent effects of the Scandinavian newcomers.

The most fruitful source of ancillary evidence for an investigation

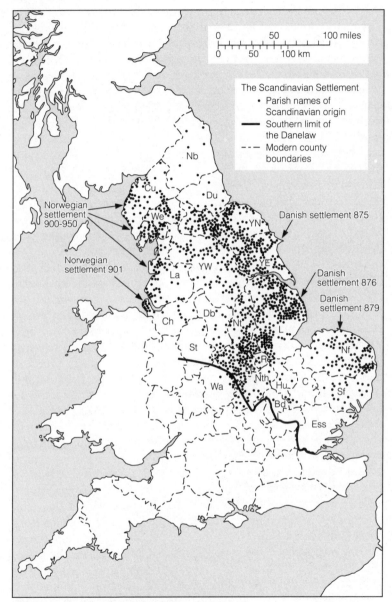

Map 2   Scandinavian settlement in England
Source: From Gwyn Jones, *A History of the Vikings* (Oxford, 1968).

of Scandinavian settlement in depth is the evidence of place-names, in itself a somewhat special and precise branch of language study. A cursory glance at the map of the parish names of England is enough to show a dramatic difference between the north and the east, 'Danish England', on the one hand, and the south and west, 'English England' on the other. North and east of the political line of demarcation established by Alfred and Guthrum in the ninth century (Watling Street and the river Lea) Scandinavian names proliferate and occasionally dominate; south and east, apart from a slight trickle into Warwickshire and Northamptonshire, they scarcely exist. Field names and minor names of all types, especially the names of streams and small rivers, reveal the speech habits of the settlers themselves, and they further reinforce firmly the simple conclusion that can be drawn from the first cursory glance. In half of England the basic settlement names were heavily modified by Scandinavian influence; the other half was virtually untouched. Within 'Danish' England itself of course the pattern, even at the superficial level, was far from uniform. In the extreme north east (Northumberland and Durham) and the south east (Essex and Hertfordshire) Danish names are few and scarce. The north west may more properly be called Norwegian than Danish, fading into a Danish area in south Lancashire to a border-county of Staffordshire where again Scandinavian names are few and concentrated mostly on the east. East Anglia, as always, is a special case with plentiful though at times ambiguous evidence of the Danish presence. Heavy concentration of Danish place-names occur in two principal areas, the territory of the Five Boroughs, and the lands dependent on the army settled at York. Over a long tract of country stretching from the mouth of the Humber through Lindsey, Nottinghamshire and Leicestershire, Danish names are thick on the ground, giving trace of the settlement achieved by armies and their followers based on the Five Boroughs of Lincoln, Stamford, Nottingham, Leicester, and to a lesser extent Derby. In the Ridings of Yorkshire (and the term 'riding' itself is Scandinavian in origin) Danish names are plentiful, notably in parts of the North and East Riding. The West Riding has not such a concentration of Danish names, except in the lower Don and around York, while Norwegian elements are powerful in Nidderdale, Calderdale and Craven. The fact of Scandinavian presence is unavoidable: the only questions that remain concern its density and intensity.

The most interesting and revealing onomastic elements are names containing the Scandinavian elements -by and -thorpe, those containing the Old English element -tun, together with a Scandinavian first element, and those representing replacements or substitutions of accredited Old English names by Scandinavian (Whitby for *Streoneshalh* and Derby for *Northworthige* are perhaps the best known of these). Modern work on these elements has enriched our knowledge by refusing to treat them merely as linguistic phenomena and by relating them firmly to the geographical, topographical and even geological reality they were meant to represent. For example, it is now generally accepted that the numerous elements in -by represent for the most part (not completely since -by remained an acceptable naming form even after the Norman Conquest) settlements established by the Danes in the first full flood of their migration in the generations after the success of their armies in the 860s and 870s. In the areas of the Five Boroughs and in Yorkshire they often represent the colonization of the best available land. Once political mastery was recognized indeed the Scandinavian settlement was in many areas juxtaposed to, not superimposed upon, the existing English villages, hamlets and farms. There was plenty of land available. In Leicestershire the main Danish settlement was made not so much in the already thickly populated valley of the Soar but in the valley of the Wreak and its tributaries. The very name of the river was changed from what was probably its English name of Eye (still used of the upper reaches) to the Danish 'Wreak', meaning 'the winding one'. Similar evidence for the setting up of colonizing groups of -bys behind the protecting hand of the armies may be discerned in Nottinghamshire and Derbyshire. These settlers could well have come along the traditional migrant route of Humber, Trent, and its tributaries with little direct impetus from the army headquarters at Nottingham, or Derby. A very heavy concentration of -bys is to be found in the Lincolnshire Wolds, and again the most intelligible explanation, borne out by dialectic study and examination of field-names is that this indicates a steady successful and early migration through the natural route of Grimsby and the mouth of the Humber. The Yorkshire evidence, taken too in conjunction with reasonable inference from dialectical and personal name customs, seems finally conclusive. The -bys, so many of which are compounded with a Danish personal name, often of an early type, are based in large part on successful colonizing ventures which were probably initiated in the last quarter of the ninth century or the early years of the tenth.

Names in -thorpe present special difficulties, so much so that some leading scholars have at times rejected them as sound evidence for early colonizing phases. They are however (like the -bys) predominantly compounded with Scandinavian elements and their number and topographical distribution speak strongly in favour of an interpretation which would see in them evidence of secondary settlement at an early stage. In Yorkshire, in particular, the name-form was often associated with settlements that concentrated on sheep-farming. The territory of the Five Boroughs presents a more complicated picture, but there again -thorpe is used of a secondary settlement, hamlet or farmstead, a dependency of a larger settlement and probably representing a later stratum in the name-giving process than the more numerous -bys. Leicestershire and Lincolnshire stand out as counties rich in -thorpes and heavily settled by Danish colonists.

To concentrate merely on the -bys and -thorpes, however, gives a somewhat misleading picture. They contain a high proportion of new settlements, good evidence indeed for a colonizing move, but far from the whole story. The Danes did not enter an empty land, nor did they clear the land of indigenous inhabitants before turning to settlement themselves. Theirs was a settlement on terms, buttressed by military power but not accompanied by wholesale massacre and eviction. Place-names survive in pure unadulterated English forms even in the most heavily Danicized areas. There also exists a substantial body of names in the Danelaw proper that contain a first element in a Danish personal name, compounded with the English element -tun (a village in a farmstead). These names are known, not completely happily but conveniently, as 'Grimston hybrids'. They have to be handled with care, but many of them represent English villages taken over and renamed by the Danes. Local circumstances determined whether -tun or -by was used in some instances, but again in general Grimston names are common in districts where there is a preponderance of English names and very few -by names. The quality of agricultural land on which the Grimstons are to be found is consistently good; the Danish names are often early or rare or both; they are more common in the westerly parts of the Danelaw (Nottinghamshire and Leicestershire) than in the east; and they may in fact well represent a very early stage in the Danish settlement when army leaders took over the lordship and initiated a degree of settlement on already favoured agricultural sites. Much of the most perceptive modern analysis attributes a priority in time to the Grimston hybrids and associates; many of the names may be associated with the earliest stages in Scandinavian settlement, even with the land-taking of the 870s.

Similar intensive work to that already done on the place-names of the Five Boroughs and of Yorkshire has not yet been done – and may indeed never be possible – on other areas of 'Danish England'. In the north west inversion compounds such as Aspatria (that is to say names consisting of a noun followed by an adjectival element (Patrick's ash tree in this instance) in Celtic order rather than normal Germanic order with preceding adjective) betray the presence of Scandinavians who have dwelt for generations among a Celtic-speaking people, residents of the Isle of Man or the Scottish Isles or Ireland, generally termed Irish/Norwegians. Other names are of pure Norwegian type and appear to have been given by colonists who moved in rapidly to these western Northumbrian lands, perhaps using the Scottish islands as mere staging posts on their journey south. The place-name structure of Cumbria, and of Cumberland in particular, however, gives an intelligible picture of early English penetration of the lowland and coastal fringe valleys where there was good arable, with the mountain heart still substantially in British hands. In the fells and dales of Cumberland and to a lesser extent Westmorland and parts of Lancashire British displacement where it occurs at all seems to have been at the hands of Scandinavian rather than Anglo-Saxon settlers. Exact work on ancillary language evidence concerning especially botanical terms substantiates the view that the special gifts of the Irish/Norwegians lay in the fields of pastoral economy, and that their shielings were newly established in the early tenth century in the upland areas where the good soil shades off into adequate or hard pasture and rock. Norwegian penetration followed the natural routes into the Pennines and the West Riding of Yorkshire: field names and dialectic forms in Dentdale in particular indicate strong Norwegian presence. As we have already seen the existence of an Irish-Norwegian kingdom at York until AD 954 makes such penetration fully intelligible, but again one must seek to oversimplify what was a very complicated human process of movement and settlement. Inversion compounds in Yorkshire itself have turned out to be largely illusory. North of the Tees, in spite of the attraction of the country around Tyneside and north to the fluctuating Scottish border there was comparatively little Scandinavian settlement, although the Danelaw in theory at least extended to the Tyne. Durham (O.E. *dun*, a hill, and

Scandinavian *holm*, an island) constitutes an important and possibly somewhat underestimated exception, where there may have been quite strong localized Danish settlement.

As we said at an earlier stage, place-name evidence in one sense constitutes no more than a specialized branch of language evidence. The study of personal names is closely associated with it, and as investigation continues into twelfth- and thirteenth-century cartulary and official government records so does the Scandinavian element in the personal-name structure of the Danelaw become increasingly apparent. There is a marked contrast again with English England where (with the exception of some boroughs) Scandinavian nomenclature is rare. Modern dialects and even more so the dialects of medieval English constitute another branch – fascinating, at times illuminating, and nearly always treacherous for the wary as well as the unwary. It is probable that great contributions will be made in future from this source towards an understanding of the nature and depth of Scandinavian settlement, but much basic work has to be done on phonology as well as semantics before the dialect material is in full fit state to be absorbed into a historical synthesis. Carefully constructed distribution maps based on the available evidence suggest an approximate line from the Solway Firth to the mouth of the Tees as the northern limit for areas of intensive settlement, while further south the lands around the Humber, north Lindsey and indeed the greater part of Yorkshire seem much more heavily influenced by Scandinavian forms than the lands of the southern Danelaw. This could seriously affect our own picture of the Scandinavian settlement, wean us away from Nottingham and Leicester, make us think more energetically of the distortions in our historical record brought about by William I's devastation of the North. Other factors, however, provide their own distorting agents to the chief picture. The strength of standard English was greater at an earlier stage for political as well as for geographical and social reasons in Mercia than in Northumbria. A dialectical border roughly from the Ribble to the Humber appeared almost as a dominant feature of the English scene in the Norman and Angevin period. Again one remembers the contrast in solidity of the Norman Conquest and feudal settlement in the land to the south of the Honours of Pontefract, Tickhill and Tutbury with the lands to the north. The tenacity of Norwegian dialect forms, strong even under sophisticated literary forms well into the fourteenth century, is a significant feature of the dialectology of parts of the north west that lie between Ribble and Mersey and spill into the Wirral peninsula. The strength of the overall linguistic evidence, in spite of obvious difficulties of interpretation and of chronology, is great and in potential even greater, but it assumes its maximum importance to the historian only when it is brought into conjunction with the powerful institutional evidence for the presence and influence of the Danes.

Institutional evidence

Much of the hardest debate of the last generation has been concerned with the density of settlement, the numbers involved, and the chronology. Linguistic and place-name evidence has properly been at the centre of the discussion, but it is also important not to neglect the institutional evidence. By the twelfth century more than a third of the country in areal extent, from the Scottish border to the line drawn by Alfred and Guthrum from Chester along Watling Street to the river Lea and London was known as the Danelaw. Was the description justified and how did the peculiarities manifest themselves?

The Danelaw, of course, as a result of the efforts of the late Old English monarchy was an integral part of the English kingdom. It was divided into shires, some like the massive Yorkshire and Lincolnshire bearing in their extent evidence of the special military and political circumstances that led to their creation. The major subdivisions made necessary by their sheer size were known under the Scandinavian name of trithings (thirds), which gives us our modern familiar 'ridings' of Yorkshire. The Midland shires, dependent on the Danish boroughs of Nottingham, Derby, and Leicester, and the shires of the south-east Danelaw conformed to the normal English pattern. So in all essentials did the great East Anglian divisions of Norfolk and Suffolk. At the time of Domesday Book, again for intelligible political reasons, the north west was still imperfectly shired but elsewhere at that very important level there was no difference between the Danelaw and the rest of England. Knights of the shire in the thirteenth century and sheriffs were similar creatures whether they hailed from Devon or Derby, Sussex or Suffolk.

Institutionally the further sub-divisions (with the exception of the 'ridings') were also similar though possibly not identical in origin or function. Over most of England, including much of the Danelaw, the principal unit was the hundred, and most of the routine fiscal and disciplinary business of the community passed through the hundred courts. In these parts of England, however, where the Scandinavian presence was the most obvious, the equivalent sub-division of a shire was known as a wapentake. The name is interesting, derived as it is through an intermediate Old English form, from the Old Norse, *vapnatak*, a term used in Scandinavian communities to signify the brandishing of weapons in an assembly to show approval (or possibly of the ceremonial taking up of weapons after an assembly or 'thing' had transacted its business). We find wapentakes in the territory of the Five Boroughs and in the greater part of Yorkshire. It is hard to be certain of significant differences in procedure from the hundred. For the moment it is enough to point to the existence of a Scandinavian name for an institution, the wapentake, that must have been the basic legal and constitutional unit for most of the inhabitants of a significant tract of England.

To be sure, the most important single body of evidence relating to the special nature of the Danelaw comes from the legal field. The Danes were a litigious people, and they and the Norwegians also had their own highly developed view of law, of legal right, and of legal institutions and procedures. Chronicles of the twelfth and thirteenth centuries recount how Danish landowners flourished in East Anglia and the Fenlands. A Ramsey writer tells how his abbey acquired lands which Cnut had taken from Englishmen to reward his followers. One estate came as compensation from Thurkill, a Dane, who had perjured himself in court and another was given by Bishop Aethelric who had got the Danish landowner drunk, had taken a wager that he could not raise the purchase price of 50 marks before dawn, and had then galloped to the king (interrupting him at a game of chess) to raise the sum successfully and in good time. These stories bear out other more prosaic records. Easterners were accustomed to the idea of Scandinavian landowners obedient in their violent way to the law. There remained, however, in England something of a contradiction and a paradox. Important modifications were made to legal practice and vocabulary; and yet the laws of Cnut which served as a model of legal utterance for the succeeding century were in the full stream of English legal achievement, in natural line of succession from the legislative activity of Edgar the Peaceful. There was, as far as one can judge, nothing approaching the juridical revolution which accompanied the Norwegian settlement of the Northern Isles and of Man.

There are perfectly intelligible reasons for this difference. Danish institutions were close to the Anglo-Saxon. Both communities had long traditions of kindred organization, wergeld payments, and of public assemblies. The only major difference lay in the field of religion, and as the Danes were converted so did the closeness of institutional life tend to become yet more intimate. Acceptance of the Christian church involved acceptance of a considerable mass of Anglo-Saxon law and custom. It also involved acceptance of a body of men – the clergy – who were the chief instruments for the written recording of law. Indeed it is possible that oral custom in the northern things and wapentakes of the Danelaw differed more than the written record will ever permit us to appreciate. Similarities in social structure and legal habit explain basic assimilation better than any attempted distinction between proud, excessively legalistic Norwegian and more complacent Dane.

From the written record itself enough has survived to point to the Danish contribution. Edgar in one of his codes expressly permitted (in 962–3) the Danes to exercise their secular rights 'according to the good laws they can best decide on'. Safeguards against theft, notably the provision of good witness (in wapentakes as well as in hundreds and boroughs) were to apply to all the nation, whether Englishmen, Danes, or Britons, but the special mention of secular right among the Danes nevertheless has great constitutional force and interest. Ethelred, in an early statement of law which he made at Wantage deep in the heart of historic Wessex, found it helpful to issue a code for the men of the Five Boroughs more or less side by side with a corresponding code 'according to the law of the English'. Private compilations in the late Anglo-Saxon period dealt with the Law of the Northumbrian People and also outlined in an elaborate detail which betrayed fear of heathenism the 'Law of the Northumbrian Priests'. Permanent basic differences may not have been effected, but the day-to-day legal practice in much of England for the greater part of the tenth and eleventh centuries was surely distinctive enough fully to merit the descriptive term the 'Danelaw' which contemporaries ascribed to it.

Some of these practices coincided well enough with Anglo-Saxon customs to be generally acceptable. Terminology in relation to land transactions suggests heavy Scandinavian influence, and it is especially interesting to note that a typical system of reliance on independent sureties (*festermen*) was invoked in the southern Danelaw in business deals connected with Peterborough estates. The presence of a public prosecutor, or *sacrabar*, though not recorded before the Conquest seems characteristic of parts of the Danelaw, spilling over into the fringe-lands of medieval Cheshire. The most valuable evidence comes from Ethelred's Wantage code (Ethelred III). Ethelred made reference in it to the twelve leading thegns in each wapentake in the land of the Five Boroughs who were to go from the court and to swear on relics that they would neither accuse any innocent person nor protect any guilty one. Arrangements were made for a majority decision (at least eight) in case of division of opinion among the twelve. These thegns constituted a virtual jury of presentment, enjoying to all appearance an element of judgement-making greater than would be found in a normal hundred. Taken together with later urban references to lawmen or *iudices* at Cambridge, Stamford, Lincoln, York, and Chester the presence of this active jury of substantial men of a territorial neighbourhood testifies to a deep and lasting contribution on the part of the Scandinavians to the permanent legal life of England.

Peculiarities in the methods of assessing fines and penalties and also in the detailed analysis of social divisions indicate some of the differences brought about by Scandinavian immigration within parts at least of the Danelaw. Antiquated units of currency (*thrymsas* in Northumbria) or Scandinavian innovations (*oras* in the territory of the Five Boroughs and the southern Danelaw generally) imply some difficulty in achieving a satisfactory basic monetary standard in the new Anglo-Scandinavian world. In Northumbria provision for a wergeld for an intermediate class of nobleman between the earls and the thegns suggest special provisions for reponsible army commanders: these men are known by the Scandinavian term 'hold'. The sustained social eminence of the free Scandinavian farmer warrior is also suggested by the simple fact that whereas in English England compensation to be paid to a lord for the death of one of his men varied in accordance with the rank of the lord, in the Danelaw the sum varied according to the dead man's status. Perhaps most important of all the technicalities is the apparent attempt to standardize fines in a way which placed a much higher premium on the king s own peace. It is always difficult to know how much weight to place on abstract legal penalties which the king would certainly have found harder to enforce in the Danelaw than in Wessex, but it does seem to be true that the king's peace was especially highly valued in the Danelaw. Efforts were also made to standardize penalties for lesser offences under the composite term *lahslit*, a penalty for the infringement of law, itself a Scandinavian word borrowed into

Anglo-Saxon. Anyone who promoted an abuse, or gave a false judgment, or simply violated just law in the Danelaw was to pay *lahslit*, assessed at the high rate of 10 half-marks for the king's thegn (higher in terms of silver pence than the standard English nobleman's fine of 120 shillings), 6 half-marks for other landowners and 12 *oras* for the freeman. Ecclesiastical offences, such as compelling a slave to work on a feast-day, refusing to pay church dues, or committing offences against a man in holy orders were also punishable by exaction of the *lahslit*. In both civil and ecclesiastical affairs the royal court was at pains to encourage rather than to suppress Danish custom. Only rarely, as when Ethelred (or more probably Archbishop Wulfstan) showed outrage at the northern custom whereby a charge of homicide brought on the day on which a victim died could not be rebutted, was any attempt made to interfere. Generally speaking Anglo-Saxon and Danish legal custom worked in reasonable harmony together.

Legal innovations and modifications in methods of achieving social discipline, ecclesiastical right and a more satisfactory landlaw were perfectly acceptable in the united Kingdom of Edgar and then of Cnut. A big social problem remains. Did the Danes introduce massive changes into the very social structure of England, and can the undoubted peculiarities of eastern England (when seen through western or southern eyes) be attributed directly to the Dane? There can be no doubt at all about some of the innovations. The basic field systems and methods of agriculture remained unchanged, though it is not too fanciful to suggest that some increasing efficiency, notably in the use of pasture land for sheep, may be Danish in origin. Methods of measurement of land and of assessment on the other hand were even more clearly altered. The process of change was not immediate nor was it uniform, but by the time of Domesday Book much of the Danelaw was assessed to public burdens not in terms of hides and yardlands (the customary units of English England) but in terms of carucates, or ploughlands, and of oxgangs or bovates. There may again be clues to deep social differences in these fiscal arrangements. The English divisions bore all the marks of an artificial system based ultimately on agrarian usage but weathered by long contact with government officers and landlords: a yardland was a quarter of a hide, a substantial notional stretch of territory amounting to as much as 30 acres in some parts of the country. The Danish divisions into carucates and bovates were that much nearer the soil, the ploughland representing the land that could be tilled by one plough-team in a year, the bovate or oxgang an eighth of a ploughland or the amount of land that could be apportioned to a farmer contributing one ox to the eight-ox plough-team. In at least three of the shires of the Danelaw, Nottingham, Lincolnshire and Norfolk, extending from the land of the Five Boroughs into East Anglia, traces are to be found of a further division, Scandinavian in name and paralleled even in Normandy, possibly equivalent to the oxgang, and that is the *manslot* or portion of allotment to one free settler. Our very full records, particularly in the northern Danelaw and in parts of East Anglia, give plentiful evidence of twelfth- and thirteenth-century methods of mensuration of assessment of land that are more Scandinavian than Anglian in origin.

Methods of accounting in general use in the north and east of England seem also to have been heavily affected by Scandinavian custom. A fondness for divisions into eight both in agrarian measurements and in currency was a dominant characteristic. The only current coin in the Danelaw as in English England remained the silver penny, but for accounting purposes larger amounts were assessed in terms of hundreds or 'long hundreds' of silver (equivalent in the early eleventh century to £8 in English money), marks, half-marks and *oras*. The most typical – and the most complicated – of these units was the *ora* which was generally reckoned to be worth 16 silver pennies. A mark consisted of 8 *oras*, and many of the sums paid as rent for mills and fisheries in the Danelaw at the time of Domesday Book still give trace of an early and fundamental system of reckoning in these units of account of 16 d. Binary reckoning came naturally to the Dane.

There remains one complicated element in the social scene that appears to offer some helpful information about the impact of the Scandinavians on English society: the nature of the peasantry in the Danelaw. Complications in interpretation occur naturally because so much of our evidence comes from Domesday Book and from later agrarian and social surveys. Throughout the Danelaw there were many marked similarities with the social structure elsewhere, with basic geographical and geological reasons determining for the most part whether or not there was a predominance of nucleated villages or hamlets or isolated farmsteads. Similar manorial arrangements were also to be found throughout England: there were lords and peasants in Dorset and in Lincolnshire. Lords, villeins, cottagers and slaves were as much a part of the social scene in Devon as in Worcester or in Yorkshire. There were, however, also some peculiarities in parts at least of the Danelaw that demand attention. English England, the south and the west, was undoubtedly more heavily manorialized than the north and the east at the time of the Norman Conquest. It was more common to find a coincidence of manor and village in English England. It was more common to find a multiplicity of manorial holdings – even up to seven or ten – in a single village in the Danelaw. In English England the manor was more firmly rooted and the lord's rights more territorialized; in the Danelaw manorial lordship and manorial rights were less onerous and more flexible. Above all there is one oddity in Domesday terminology which has occasioned much comment and discussion. The Domesday scribes used five principal terms to describe the peasantry: villeins, cottars (or bordars), slaves, freemen and sokemen. The line between freemen and sokemen is slight and hard to distinguish, connected partly with the legal obligations owed by the sokemen, partly by the legal obligations laid on the land possessed by the sokemen, and partly, one suspects, by the customs of the neighbourhood and by the scribal practice of those making the circuit returns for the Domesday Commissioners. Both groups may fairly be taken together in that they stand out against the other manorial peasantry. Freemen and sokemen had direct responsibility in matters concerning suit of court and payment of geld where the manorial peasants were fully dependent on their lords. It is the distribution of these freemen and sokemen which has prompted the deepest discussion. In substantial numbers they are to be found only north and east of Watling Street, only in other words in the Danelaw. Sokemen account for roughly half the recorded population in Lincolnshire. Freemen make up over 40 per cent of the recorded population in Norfolk and Suffolk. Yorkshire is a special case because of the devastation caused by William's Harrying of the North and the subsequent depreciation of peasant status, but even there firm traces remain of a greater general freedom among the peasantry. The point is firmly made by a contrast between the Domesday figures for Warwickshire and Leicestershire, counties not dissimilar in agrarian background, Warwickshire to the south and west of Watling Street in English England and its neighbour Leicestershire to the east and north in the Danelaw. Recorded populations are roughly the same, but while Leicestershire has more than a third of its population described as sokemen there are only a handful so recorded in Warwickshire. Can such a contrast be explained away as a mere difference in terminology or does it betray a social distinction of fundamental importance in the history of the English peasantry?

Most historians would agree that the presence of sokemen and freemen in significant numbers does in fact betray deep differences in society, even after some discount is allowed for regional differences, such as the recording or non-recording of a free rent-paying peasantry, on the part of the Domesday scribes. Such presence points to the firmer hold of lordship on land and community in English England, and to the more intensive manorialization of the south and west. There rests one further question vital to our present investigation, and that is quite simply how directly, if at all, is the existence of this free element in English society to be associated with the Scandinavians? Some of our finest historians have made the connection strong and direct. Sir Frank Stenton suggested that the freemen and the sokemen of the east at the time of Domesday Book were substantially the descendants of free Danish settlers, of the men of the ninth-century armies who shared out the lands of Northumbria, East Mercia and East Anglia, or of their later followers and dependants. Peculiarities of land tenure, notably in East Anglia, have been associated with Scandinavian complexities where the relative freedom of a land market in newly developed territories was in conflict with Scandinavian notions of odal-right and family land. Peculiarities in definition of legal rights have been associated with the tenacity of the litigious Dane in his emphasis on the attendance of the local thing and folk-moot. Other historians have warned us instead to handle our Dane with care, to pay more attention to the question of agrarian prosperity, and to remember our ignorance of the differences in regional social structure in pre-Danish England. Some of the peculiarities of East Anglian society, for example, have been traced back to very early times and even ascribed to Frisian contacts in the days of primary Anglo-Saxon settlement. English freemen existed in significant numbers in the East Anglia of King Edmund and in the East Anglia ruled by Guthrum the converted Dane. On balance it does seem desirable not to swing to an extreme nor to reject the importance of the Scandinavian element. So many fields of evidence, linguistic and social, substantiate the bare political record. It is proper however to stress that both direct and indirect effects led to the creation of the free element in the Danelaw. The direct effects are self-evident, the infusion of large numbers of Scandinavian farmer warriors with their traditions of independence, reinforced by their nature as colonists. It is doubtful, however, if these traditions would be strong enough to survive for four or five generations when subject to the political pressures and upheavals which afflicted all of Britain in the tenth and eleventh centuries. The indirect effects are a different matter. Danish conquest under Guthrum and his contemporaries brought a savage dislocation to land tenure throughout the Danelaw. Royal lands and ecclesiastical lands could not survive the onslaught. Even after the recovery and conversion in the early tenth century royal wealth did not recover its former position and the church remained notoriously impoverished. The archbishopric of York was so poor that for two long periods it was held in plurality with the wealthy southern see of Worcester. It has long been an axiom of medieval studies that where one finds a wealthy church there also is a dependent peasantry. The dislocation caused in the Danelaw by the Danish success, no matter how swift the personal conversion, was clearly tremendous. As Christianity became again the dominant religion of the countryside so were fresh endowments made, and often – a special feature of the Danelaw – parish churches would be set up by groups of moderately prosperous freemen. By the time of the Norman Conquest the new Benedictine abbeys in the southern Danelaw and the ministers of York, Beverley, Ripon and Southwell were beginning to exhibit the features of wealthy ecclesiastical corporations. The effects of the break in continuity were nevertheless deep and enduring. At the period of growth and colonization no well established lords, lay or ecclesiastical, were present ready and able to take the lead in new settlement and so to augment their own dominical authority. Many of the Danish army leaders, kings and jarls initially, earls and *holds* in the second phase of settlement, did extremely well out of the venture but they did not dominate the countryside as a bishop of Worcester or a great thegn or ealdorman of the south could dominate people and land. Considerable weight needs to be given to this break in the line of lordship and tenure if any full explanation of the curious social structure of the Danelaw is to be achieved.

To this point emphasis has properly been placed on Scandinavian influences on the rural society of the Danelaw. Most recent concern has centred on the problem of numbers, on the question of the density and intensity of the settlements. Were the Scandinavian elements that we can isolate so clearly in rural society the outcome of initial conquest and early heavy settlement or did they emerge as a natural product of a further period of intense colonization in the tenth century? The balance of evidence seems at the moment to weigh in favour of the first of these two views. This is not to deny a measure, in some areas a considerable measure, of internal colonization between AD 950 and 1066 by a population that can legitimately be called Anglo-Scandinavian. Monastic history as well as our more prosaic world of government activity, administration, coinage and law reminds us that the last century of Anglo-Saxon England was a time of growth and expansion internally in the economy. Archæological evidence from Denmark itself provides thought-provoking parallels. Traces of so-called 'magnate-houses' in the tenth century suggest movement towards something approaching a manorial economy, a development which fits easily with our own recognized consolidation of a thegnly class in tenth-century England. Scandinavian place-names can on this basis be interpreted not so much in terms of an extension of settlement as a break-up of older greater estates into separate ownership. We still face the problem of where the individual owners came from. To go to an extreme and to deny the presence of Scandinavian settlers in substantial numbers in the period *c*.870–920 would seem to belittle the relatively clearcut evidence of linguistic, onomastic, institutional and indeed political history.

There remains one further important and sometimes neglected dimension to the Danish problem. Because so much of the vital evidence comes from the carefully kept records of conscientious late eleventh- and twelfth-century landlords historians have tended to concentrate on the countryside, on the Danish farmers of Yorkshire and Lincolnshire, the Grimms, Thorgeirrs, Osketills and Svartbrands of Kirkdale, Helperby, Lazenby or Conisbrough. There is therefore a danger of neglecting one of the principal contributions made by the Scandinavians, namely the stimulus given to urban development. We have from time to time talked of Danish traders, of continued contacts with the Scandinavian homeland, of continuous mobility by sea from the Northern Isles along the east coast of England to London, Kent, and round to the Isle of Wight and beyond. The tenth-century attempt to establish a kingdom with pivotal centres at Dublin and York failed: it was remarkable and significant enough that such an attempt should be made. There are consequences of all this activity which should not be ignored. Unlike the Anglo-Saxons who seemed to forget what nautical skill they ever possessed soon after landing in these islands, the Scandinavians retained their skill at sea. Their principal settlements, well fortified and under military control for at least the first generation, developed into thriving trading towns. In Northumbria York quickly grew into one of the main urban centres of England. By the end of the Anglo-Saxon period its population approached 10,000, and indeed one contemporary source estimated the number of people in York, the 'metropolis of the Northumbrians', at an incredible (and false) figure of 30,000, not counting children and youths. The city was said to be full and wealthy beyond words with the riches of merchants who came from all sides, specially from the Danish people. Excavations at the Coppergate site near the confluence of the Foss and the Ouse gave evidence of burgeoning prosperity in the early tenth century with houses and workshops on planned sites, industrial activity in metal, leather, and wood, specialized moneyers at their mint with dies and lead trial pieces, and full trace of the wide-ranging international dimension of the commercial life of York. The brilliant reconstruction of tenth-century Coppergate on permanent show at the Jorvik Viking Centre gives superb insight into the physical nature, the busyness, language, sights and smells of Viking York.

Lincoln also thrived mightily and under the Anglo-Scandinavian kings York and Lincoln became the administrative headquarters for the two largest shires in terms of areal extent in the whole of the English kingdom. Lincoln was one of the 'Five Boroughs', and three others, Nottingham, Derby, and Leicester also became important permanent administrative headquarters, the chief towns of their shires. The fifth of the group, Stamford, was in a special situation, something of a border borough as far as administrative arrangements were concerned, but still an important commercial centre in late Anglo-Saxon England. Further south in the Danelaw urban development was not negligible though complicated to some extent by the Benedictine revival of the late tenth century which brought ultimate importance to Peterborough, Ely, and Bury St Edmunds. Thetford, Cambridge and Norwich all show features of urban growth that owe much directly to the Scandinavian presence.

Naturally we must be careful not to attribute all urban growth to the Scandinavians. Historians are becoming increasingly aware that the second half of the tenth century and the first half of the eleventh experienced economic changes which led to the establishment of permanent town life in large tracts of the old Carolingian empire and in England. Many of the boroughs set up as defensive positions by Alfred and his son and daughter (though by no means all) also developed into English towns with permanent urban life. Fortunately we have one means of measuring the extent of Scandinavian influence on urban growth, inexact statistically but nonetheless important and significant in its way. The creation of an efficient silver coinage was one of the outstanding achievements of the late Old English monarchy. Particularly after the reforms of Edgar the standard of the sometimes very beautiful silver pennies was systematically maintained and an elaborate administrative process established by which central royal control was imposed through issue of dies, at times from a central die-cutting office at London, by regular changes in type of coinage, and by savage legal penalties against abuse of dies and false coining. The actual striking of coins was carried out in a multiplicity of mints (over seventy have been identified) by moneyers who were men of substance and standing, sometimes possessing their own rights of jurisdiction over dependants. These moneyers placed their own names on the reverse of the coins, together with the name of the mint. Full statistical information will be lacking until all Anglo-Saxon coins have been properly published – a massive undertaking as will be readily appreciated when it is realized that there are many thousand coins of the reign of Ethelred known from finds in the Island of Gotland alone. Statistical information, complete or incomplete, in this field has always to be handled with care: no one loses coins if he can help it and the historian can deal, unhappily, only with coins that have been lost. Even so, the impressions that are already given by the samples of published coins available are so powerful that it is hard to see anything more than a spurious exactness coming from ultimate complete statistical analysis. The mints of the Danelaw contain many, often a majority, of men bearing Scandinavian names among the moneyers; in English England with few exceptions (complex London had its Scandinavian group and Chester its Irish/Norwegian elements) English names are dominant and often virtually exclusive. In sheer quantity of coins also the mints of the Danelaw contributed rather more than might be expected to the tally of surviving coins. London was undoubtedly the most prolific of the English mints and the principal trading centre. Of the next three in order of size two were Danelaw mints, York and Lincoln – and York and Lincoln contend with Winchester in the top group of mints throughout the reigns of Ethelred, Cnut and Edward the Confessor. There was also a small group of five or six prolific mints of the second order, and Stamford ranks here side by side with Chester and Bristol and Exeter and Canterbury. The evidence of the coins points unmistakably to the importance of the Danelaw boroughs in the commercial life of England, and to the importance of a very strong Scandinavian element within the Danish boroughs.

London was naturally a special case. The importance of London grew disproportionately to the growth of the rest of the country between say 980 and 1066. For a period of time in Alfredian England London was under Viking control and the Thames estuary continued to be an attraction for Scandinavian traders and raiders throughout the tenth century. We have seen how prominent a part London played in the Danish wars of the reign of Ethelred. Under Cnut the Scandinavians intensified their role in the trading life of the community. Viking finds, including runic inscriptions and sculpture in typical Scandinavian style, testify to their presence. The principal routine courts for handling commercial difficulties came to be known as hustings (or *hus-things*). Many early dedications to St Olaf, some of which may have been given soon after the saint's death, give positive proof of the existence of coherent groups of Scandinavians living within the city, Christian and established, yet maintaining awareness of their origins. Privileges which certainly date back to the reign of Cnut continued to be enjoyed at London by Scandinavian merchants well into the twelfth century.

In conclusion it may be said that the Scandinavian impact on England resulted in a thorough enrichment of the community. Intensification of agrarian effort brought it about that by 1066 Lincolnshire, Norfolk and Suffolk ranked high among the prosperous shires of England. Scandinavian contribution to the political life of the country had been great at all levels, from the monarchy itself where Cnut ranks as one of the most successful of English rulers to the minor administrative divisions of the Danelaw and the hustings and courts of doomsmen of London, York, and Chester. The opening up of the North Sea to regular commerce proved permanent and was not disrupted by the Norman Conquest. Above all the impact of these active seafaring Northerners on the early life and stabilization of the towns of north and eastern England was tremendous. York appears in saga stories as an impressive town where the Scandinavian language and institutions were fully familiar. The importance of the Scandinavian element in London has probably been underestimated. Regionally and generally the influx of the Scandinavians made a vital contribution to the inner nature of the English communities of the Middle Ages.

The Celtic world

The effects of the Scandinavian invasions on the Celtic communities in Britain differed to a considerable extent from the effects on England. Accidents of geography made it more of a Norwegian venture than a Danish and there is not the same urgency for land-taking in Britain that one senses in the Danish moves. The Norwegian population was smaller and its surplus smaller still. Even so the population of Shetland alone seems to have exceeded 20,000 by the end of the Viking Age, and conservative estimates of Iceland's total population at the same period suggest a figure of over 50,000. The most intense Norwegian colonizing enterprises were undertaken in relation to the Northern Isles, to the Faroes, pre-eminently to Iceland and more exotically to Greenland and to Vinland on the North American coast. This sombre Northern background is forgotten at peril if one wishes to read a just evaluation of Scandinavian settlement in Celtic Britain and Ireland.

The Northern Isles themselves were of course completely Scandinavianized. The language spoken in Orkney and Shetland from the end of the Viking period is generally referred to as Norn and was completely West Scandinavian, close to Norwegian. Such is the nature of island settlements that distinctions can fairly be made between the Norn of Orkney and that of Shetland, and the nature of the origin of the settlements can be deduced from these distinctions. For example, while it is generally true that settlements into the northern islands came predominantly from the west and south-west coasts of Norway, Shetland Norn bears its strongest affinities with the dialects of the south west with its focal point in the Stavanger area. Orkney Norn seems closer, though marginally only, to areas a shade further east, from Stavanger to modern Kristiansand. It is a delicate point that serves to enliven the somewhat arid pages of linguistic analysis to find a conclusion that has Orkney peopled from Kristiansand and Shetland from Stavanger; and in fact language evidence, reinforced by archaeological evidence, tells us firmly that these conclusions concern only predominant groups. Norwegians from the whole littoral from Trondheim to Oslo took part in the enterprise: but the predominating element in the settlement was indeed from south west and the west, from the Sogn and the Hardanger in particular as well as from the heartlands of Rogaland and the south.

The language itself continued to dominate throughout the Middle

Ages. There was little impact from Gaelic but English (or more precisely Scottish English) began to have an influence in the later Middle Ages, probably not seriously until the fifteenth century. Political circumstances determined some change. The last of the great Norse earls was Ragnald (Rægnvold) who died in 1158, though the line lingered on until 1231. They were succeeded by Scottish earls from the mainland, of the line of Angus (1231-1321), Strathearn (1321-79) and Sinclair (from 1379). Their nominal allegiance rested with Norway, or, as it became, the joint kingdom of Norway-Denmark. The political links with Scandinavia were finally broken in 1468-9 when allegiance passed from Christian I of Denmark/ Norway to James III of Scotland. The Sinclairs and after them the Scottish kings and earls represented a strong Scotticizing agency, in the respect of language, of course, an Anglicizing agent. Norn remained the common speech of Orkney throughout the sixteenth century, and the Orcadians were probably mostly bilingual throughout the seventeenth. It was not until the end of the eighteenth century that the language suffered seriously and then its disappearance was rapid. English was too strong, too useful, and too close in structure for Norn to survive into the more mobile world of the modern age. Shetland was more conservative, particularly in the remotest of the islands and as late as the 1890s Scandinavian scholars were still able to collect from living memory and use more than 10,000 words and phrases of Scandinavian origin. Even more impressive is the nature of the place-name evidence. In Shetland alone the Scandinavian scholar Jakob Jakobsen, distinguished more than 50,000 names of Old Norse origin, and modern investigators put this figure as an underestimate. The overwhelming majority of historic farmnames in Orkney is of Old Norse origin, and a figure as high as 99 per cent has been suggested and not seriously challenged. There are literally hundreds of Old Norse place-name elements to be distinguished in this mass of names. Among the most common and interesting forms, many of which are also found in mainland Britain, may be mentioned the following Old Norse elements: *bolstaðr* (farm – usually in the modern form -bister); *setr* (house or homestead); *sætr* (shieling); *staðr* (plural *staðir*: place, site, or often farm settlement, in modern place-names often reduced to -*sta* or -*ster* or in Orkney modified to -*ston*); *borg* (a fortification); *by (r)* (in the Northern Isles 'farm' not as in the Danelaw from Danish -*by* meaning 'village'); *skali* (hut or shed, but often in Orkney 'hall'); *kvi* (enclosure for cattle – in modern form – quoy); *garðr* (enclosure). Natural features and especially words connected with the sea and the coast are of almost exclusively Old Norse origin (for example the familiar *ey* (island), *nes* (promontory), and *vik* (bay or inlet), and the not quite so familiar *hamarr* (rock, wall of rock), *mynni* (mouth of river), and *vagr* (creek or bay as in modern Kirkwall or Osmundwall or Snarravoe).

Institutional evidence confirms, if confirmation is needed, the story told by the structure of the language and the place-names. Methods of settling local disputes, the solemn rules of the assemblies or 'things', the system of taxation based closely on Norwegian practice, the units of taxation and the terminology, the equation of the proceeds of taxation with provision of ships for defence are only a few among the many institutional features of the Northern Isles that tell of Scandinavian customs and Scandinavian inhabitants. Strong though it is, the institutional evidence needs to be handled with care. Our knowledge of it comes from later sources and there is a sense in which it is particularly naïve to express surprise that communities that bore allegiance to Scandinavian kings and princes for over half a millennium should enjoy a Scandinavian type of institutional life. · The economy was similar, the social life based on the sea and the sheep-farm almost identical. Special characteristics, such as the nature of the water-mills tell also of a Norwegian affinity. Taken together with the language and the place-names the institutions of Orkney and Shetland point to one inescapable conclusion. The Northern Isles represent in their medieval being a firm testimony to the success of a colonizing venture undertaken by Norwegians in the Viking Age, on a par with the settlement of the Faroes and of Iceland, a touchstone and a contrast to the rest of Britain.

For when we turn to the rest of the Celtic World, the mainland of much of the Highlands of Scotland, the Hebrides, the southern Scottish islands, part of the mainland of south-west Scotland, the Isle of Man, Ireland and Wales, we find plentiful evidence of Scandinavian presence but nothing resembling the complete Scandinavianization so characteristic of Orkney and Shetland. We miss the clearcut language evidence of Norn and face difficulties different in kind but as great in their way as those that faced us in consideration of the impact of Scandinavian language elements on English. Again, however, language and place-names offer the first field for examination. The Celtic languages are very different in structure, vocabulary and stress from the Germanic. Wherever a sizeable population survived (in other words virtually everywhere in the Celtic West) the native language tended to survive side by side with Scandinavian in clear duality rather than in symbiosis. Even so the effects of the presence of Scandinavian speakers had varying impact on the Celtic-speaking communities, and the many variations themselves tell us much of the degree of Scandinavian influence.

It is now generally agreed that Scottish Gaelic is directly descended from the language spoken by immigrants into Argyll from northeast Ireland (Dalriada) towards the end of the fifth century AD. There was no serious divergence from the language of the Irish homeland until at least the tenth century, and most would say that even as late as the thirteenth century they were still essentially one language, common Gaelic as it is sometimes called. This is not to say that there was not intense local divergence in speech from part to part of the Gaelic-speaking world, but essentially there was only one language in that world throughout the Middle Ages: Ireland and the Highlands formed a single culture-province. Their unity was demonstrated and to some extent preserved by the attachment of the learned literate classes to the common Gaelic tongue, admittedly as the early modern period progressed more and more a literary language increasingly antiquated and divorced from the living, diverging, spoken Gaelic tongues of Ireland and Scotland. The Gaelic tongue of Man was part of the unified group and its spoken version continued to be close to Scottish Gaelic certainly until the end of the Middle Ages. Dramatic sound changes in the fifth and sixth centuries and less spectacular modifications up to at least AD 1000 were shared in common by the whole group. Differentiations, mostly in the degree to which changes were accepted, begin to occur between the tenth and the thirteenth centuries and slowly a spoken Eastern Gaelic (Scottish and Manx) comes to be distinguished from Western Gaelic or Irish. After the thirteenth century the two groups cease to share innovation in common except for rare coincidence and after the fifteenth century Eastern Gaelic sees further decisive differentiation within itself between Scottish Gaelic and Manx.

We now have to face directly the very complicated question of Norse influence on Gaelic. Language in this respect mirrors faithfully political developments. The Norwegian king, Magnus Barefoot, had asserted his lordship over Shetland, Orkney, the Hebrides, Anglesey and Man in the course of his dramatic and full-scale expedition of 1098. Not all his gains were permanent, but he made a treaty with Edgar, king of the Scots (1097–1107) which provided the formal basis for the constitutional situation in the islands for much of the Middle Ages. Magnus was recognized as lord of the isles with the right to the allegiance of the local rulers. He made no claim to the mainland (apart from Kintyre), although there were Norse rulers in much of the North, in Caithness, Ross, and Sutherland. The main lines of political development in the succeeding century and a half consisted of Scottish attempts with reasonable success to make a reality of their lordship of the North and Norwegian failure to make a reality of their lordship of the West. The independence of the 'kings' of the islands became legendary, though from time to time the lordship of Norway in civil matters concerning tribute and in ecclesiastical matters (particularly after the setting up of the archbishopric at Nidaros in the early 1150s) was fully recognized. Haakon IV in 1266 made one final effort to impose strong Norwegian control, was defeated by the Scottish king (and the weather) at the battle of Largs in the October and died in Orkney on his way home. The resulting Treaty of Perth set the seal on island constitutional history for the succeeding two centuries. The Hebrides and the Isle of Man passed into Scottish hands in return for a payment of 4,000 marks and an annual render of 100 marks. Scottish lordship did not in fact prove much more effective than Norwegian. The Isle of Man passed into English control in the fourteenth century. In the Islands themselves authority rested with the lords of the isles, chieftains (MacDougalls and later MacDonalds) in direct descent from the twelfth-century Scandinavian adventurer and jarl Somerled. Effective Scottish control had to wait in large measure until the sophisticated days of James VI (James I of England) in the early seventeenth century.

During all these centuries of turmoil there was constant contact between Gaelic and Scandinavian speakers. There was a long bilingual period which lasted certainly to the thirteenth century and probably longer. In the event the Norsemen became Gaelic-speakers in the Hebrides and also where they settled in the Highlands. It seems likely (and this again makes sound political sense) that the thirteenth century was the decisive point in which Eastern Gaelic separated off from Western. And the Norse influence, especially in place-names and in general vocabulary, is one of the distinguishing marks between Eastern and Western Gaelic, between Scottish and Irish. The vast majority of the present Gaelic place-names in the Outer Hebrides, especially Lewis, are of ultimate Norse origin. In the Inner Hebrides the proportion is still high and has been estimated at 60 per cent in Skye and about a third in Islay. The contrast with

Ireland in this respect is startling, for hardly any Norse names of Irish places have been taken over into Irish. On the mainland of Scotland they have left evidence of their presence both in pure Norse forms and in forms that have been taken over into Gaelic: *ob* (bay), *vidh* (a ford), *dail* (field), *sgol* (rinse or wash), *strome* (a current or stream), are among the most obvious of the place-name elements. Borrowings into vocabulary include common words such as *lagh* (law), *nabaidh* (neighbour), *stailinn* (steel), *biota* (a churn), and *geodha* (a creek): these are common to Manx as well as to Scottish but do not appear in Irish. Some of the most intimate and intricate sound changes, common to Scottish Gaelic and Manx, seem also attributable to Old Norse influence. The Isle of Man was a special case, and Manx Gaelic suffered severely from heavy Anglo-Norman pressure throughout the critical twelfth and thirteenth centuries; even so, a sizeable minority of Manx place-names (probably about one in six) are wholly or partly of ultimate Scandinavian origin, and the vocabulary of Manx Gaelic has preserved a few Scandinavian borrowings (*spret* (start), *grinney* (a gate), and *oalsun* (a rope from head to foreleg of a cow)) not to be found in its Scottish sister language. Brilliant archaeological work in Man which has made us familiar with Viking boat-shaped long houses, with Viking graves (including the important boat burial at Balladoole), and Viking ornamentation in the full Ringerike and Urnes styles, has made the Scandinavian presence tangible and intelligible as in few parts of the British Isles. The practice of boat burial, not commonly recorded in the British Isles, and even a possible example of suttee remind us of the intensity of the social impact from an early stage. On the whole the evidence is consistent for Man as for the Hebrides and the Highlands. Gaelic and Scandinavian languages were spoken in close conjunction for at least four centuries and had important structural influences the one on the other.

Institutional evidence for the impact of Scandinavian settlement is also plentiful along the Celtic West. Again the Northern Isles are in a category of their own, their institutional life thoroughly Scandinavian in all respects. They provide the centre and focal point for all moves to a more thorough political and social Scandinavianization of the western seaboard of Britain. On the mainland of Scotland effects were more spasmodic and less long-lasting. The name Dingwall (*Thing-vollr*, place of assembly and presumably administrative headquarters) serves to remind us that at its height Scandinavian political influence was paramount throughout much of Scotland to the north of the Great Glen. Dingwall is no more than a dozen miles from modern Inverness. The north-east Scottish coast was surely the preserve of Scandinavian fleets ranging from the Northern Isles base, and for a long period a Scandinavian *jarl* exercised authority in Caithness, at times subservient to the earls of the isles, at times virtually independent, and at other times again subordinate if not subservient to the Scottish kings. The mainland, however, came fully under Scottish control before the end of the Middle Ages with the result that fewer signs are to be found there than in the isles of Scandinavian institutional influence. Elsewhere it is a different matter. The taxation system and accompanying administrative divisions established in the Viking Age and confirmed and reinforced by Norwegian kings and earls in the twelfth and thirteenth century have left a permanent mark on the Northern and Western Isles and Man. In constitutional theory they were administered by the earl of Orkney who exacted tribute, two-thirds of which was to go to the king while he (or men acting for him) was to take the other third. This overall scheme was common to the Scandinavian world, and analogies have been found with the Baltic earldoms, especially on the Isle of Gotland, that were subordinate to the Swedish crown. Even more striking analogies have been found with the administrative systems erected to make the tribute-taking possible. They are closely related to the familiar Norwegian institution of *leidang*, that is to say a taxation system arranged so as to provide the lord and ruler with a suitable well-manned, and well-equipped fleet. Orkney for example was divided into six districts called *husaby* districts, with a *husaby* estate in each, that is to say a farm to which tribute would be brought in proper season. The *husaby* districts were further divided into 36 units called *urisland*, and they in turn were subdivided into quarters known as *skattlands*. The system seems complicated but may in fact have been simple and effective. The name *skattland* (scot-paying land) is in itself revealing and represents the basic family farm set up when free settlers took land. Each *husaby* district in Orkney contained 144 *skattlands* which may well have been referred to as a 'long hundred' (a duodecimal 'hundred' of 12 × 12). It is further possible that the 144 tax-paying units went to further the construction and maintenance of four ships (with 36 oars apiece): in origin at least levy service would be expected from each of these basic units. If we turn to the bigger unit, the *urisland*, again the term itself is informative. It means literally an 'ounce' land, that is to say territory contributing a standard ounce of silver at the time of the annual levying of tax or tribute. From the central earldom of Orkney this would amount to 144 ounces of silver to the Norwegian king a year and 72 ounces to the earl. Relationship with the systems in force in the Scandinavian homeland is direct and immediate. In spite of differences in terminology the taxation and administrative systems in force in the Hebrides and in the Isle of Man appear to have been identical. In the Hebrides divisions known as *tirungs* corresponded to the *urislands* and they again were divided into quarters. In the Isle of Man the analogy is even more exact. The island was divided into 6 sheadings (an Old West Scandinavian word *settungr*, a sixth). Each sheading was divided into 36 *treens* and these again were split up into four *quarterlands*. The *quarterland* (like the *skattland*) constituted the basic unit of levy. It may well be also, an analogy with Scandinavian custom, that the *treens* (or *urislands* or *tirungs*) had the basic responsibility in the early days of the conversion for the provision of a small chapel (or *Keill*) and that this responsibility later developed into the duty of looking after parts of the bigger churches which in time replaced the early chapels. Some of these administrative arrangements may be traced back to pre-Viking days and indeed be fundamental to the first ordering of territorial government in the Scottish kingdom of the ninth century. But it would seem rash to deny the Norseman a major part in the final shaping of the government system of administration and taxation in the lands which lay completely under their nominal control until at least 1266.

Ireland

The Irish situation is different in nature and in degree from the Scottish and the Manx. The defeat at Clontarf in 1014 did not lead to the expulsion of the Scandinavians. They continued to live and to trade and fight and even to recruit from Scandinavia proper and from the Islands. Clontarf nevertheless had a direct effect on their development. The defeat marks an end of any Scandinavian hopes (no matter how fleeting and illusory) of forming a coherent territorial kingdom or earldom that would incorporate large tracts of countryside. It marks a decisive stage in the localization of Scandinavian settlement in Ireland.

There were, of course, indications even before Clontarf that this was a strong element in Irish/Scandinavian history. Expansionist schemes in the tenth century had been directed strongly eastwards across the Irish Sea into north-west England and over the Pennines to York. In no part of Europe – though there are possible analogies along the Waterways of Russia – did the Vikings concentrate so clearly on their fortified settlements and quaysides along the coast. Dublin, Waterford, Wexford, Cork and Limerick remained their headquarters, sometimes under Scandinavian dynasties, sometimes subject directly to native Irish rulers. After the Anglo-Norman Conquest in the early 1170s these settlements were subsumed in the greater Angevin empire. The Ostmen (men from the east) enjoyed a precarious independence in social matters for another century or so but were of no further consequence in the political history of Ireland.

The direct effects of the Vikings on Irish society are therefore not as great as one might expect. They have left a scatter of vocabulary, notably in matters concerning the sea and ships and commerce, but not nearly as much as in Scottish Gaelic. Indeed some of the Norse influence on Irish Gaelic has been explained by immigration from the Islands and the Highlands across the North Channel into Ulster and the north east as far south as Louth and North Meath. Language authorities date these modifications primarily to the period between the fourteenth and the end of the sixteenth century. Norse influence on place-names is also relatively localized, again much less widespread and deep than in the Scottish Gaelic areas.

We must not nevertheless attempt to underwrite and to minimize the indirect effects of the Vikings. Politically they helped to accelerate a natural movement in balance from the centre towards the east. Throughout the century and a half that separated Clontarf from the Anglo-Norman invasion they remained a dominant power on the Irish Sea. They were the great traders of the western seaboard during this age. Their coinage, modelled on English example in the last decade of the tenth century, helped to formalize and ease trading ventures from Ireland into England, particularly along their two well-beaten routes that led to Chester and to Bristol. Dublin, Wexford and Waterford provided important staging points that linked the mobile men of the North with settled England. Above all there should be no denigration of the part they played in increasing the wealth of Ireland and in establishing firmly the beginnings of urban institutional life. As specialist boat-builders, sailors and traders they seem to have been somewhat encapsulated as far as ordinary Irish society was concerned. Excavation by archaeologists, notably in High Street and Winetavern Street, Dublin, has helped to give a realistic picture of the state of urban material development, enough to indicate that a high degree of material comfort had been achieved.

The ecclesiastical life of Ireland was radically altered in the course of the late eleventh and early twelfth centuries; and the coastal settlements played a vital part in events that led to a measure of reform and a complete overhaul of the diocesan system. English influences came in heavily through the Scandinavian towns, especially through Dublin. Lanfranc, archbishop of Canterbury (1070–89) took it as a vital part of his duty to extend as far as it was possible the hold of his metropolitan church over the Irish Christians, and it was the see of Dublin that saw the strongest of his ventures. Bishop Patrick (d. 1084) was consecrated by Lanfranc and so was his successor Donatus (d. 1095). Archbishop Anselm had the same basic aspirations and consecrated Bishop Samuel (d. 1121). Oaths of obedience were exacted from these men in conformity to the custom of Canterbury. Anselm further consecrated Malchus as the first bishop of Waterford in 1096. All these men were Irishmen trained in England, and at a great reforming Synod held in 1111 it is notable that Dublin was not included among the Irish sees because its bishops were subject to Canterbury. Ecclesiastical practice in this respect surely reflected social reality. The world of the Hiberno-Norse townsmen and traders was more akin to England than to Gaelic Ireland. Reform came to the Irish church partly through the Hiberno-Norse bishops but partly also through sheer pressure of Hildebrandine ideas largely disseminated through the English church. Both Lanfranc and Anselm were concerned, as their voluminous correspondence shows, with the state of the Irish church. Charges of laxness in the imposition of marriage laws, of the uses in procedures for episcopal consecration and of church ceremony were freely made. By the early twelfth century the Papacy itself was represented by its own legate, possibly first by Ua-Dunain, the bishop of the Meath, and thereafter certainly by Gilbert, bishop of Limerick who resigned his charge to St Malachy in 1140. At the Synod of Kells in 1152, Dublin itself was brought fully into the Irish fold and recognized as an archbishopric under the primacy of Armagh. Cardinal John Paparo brought *pallia* for the four archbishops, Armagh, Cashel, Dublin, and Tuam, with express recognition of the primacy of Armagh. Canterbury had indeed failed to secure permanent control, but its influence, particularly through the Hiberno-Norse bishoprics, was considerable.

In spite of the obvious importance of the Hiberno-Norse element in commercial and religious life it remains true to say that the ultimate impact of the Vikings on the political moulding of Ireland remained less formidable than on Man, the Islands and the Highlands. The reason for this is partly to be found in the later chequered history of Ireland. The Anglo-Norman conquest of more than half the island brought about changes, in language, social structure and religious organizations that in one respect consummated the possible patterns hinted at in Hiberno-Norse developments and completely overshadowed it. Most of all however the reason is to be found in the nature of the settlements themselves. During these centuries permanence went with the land. The traders and sailors of Dublin and Waterford did not bring the permanent marks of the settler and colonizer into Irish society.

Wales

The effects of the Viking invasions on Wales present a different picture again from that which we have seen elsewhere in the Celtic world. There are resemblances to the situation in Ireland but there is one big contrast. There is no certain evidence that a substantial Viking fortified centre on the scale of Dublin or Waterford was established in Wales. It is possible, indeed probable, that for substantial periods of time Norse-speaking men built up settlements that were meant to be permanent in Pembrokeshire and in several favoured seaports along the South Welsh coast; but these were small-scale, purposeful, almost one might say vocational. They were connected with Hiberno-Norse control of sea-routes and trading ventures into England by means of the Bristol Channel. Even more so than in Ireland the seamen lacked a territorial base. There was no mastery of the hinterland and without that permanent impress was impossible in the Viking centuries.

The reasons for this state of affairs are relatively simple to analyse and we have already in an earlier chapter discussed the political situation which led to successful Welsh resistance at critical moments when serious colonizing settlement might have been attempted. Indeed if the full perspective of Scandinavian settlement is taken into account it will readily be seen that the colonizing thrust necessarily grows weaker the further south the longships have to travel. There was only a limited supply of manpower. Along the south-western route the Norwegians settled lustily in the Northern Isles, the Hebrides, and Man. Ireland attracted but in the end at Clontarf repelled; and the Welsh situation was even more unfavourable without adequate human resources to sustain it. From time to time and most notably at the very end of the Viking Age proper attempts were made to bring at least Anglesey fully into the Hiberno-Norse world. Long tradition, association with Man (the Menevian islands of antiquity), accessibility from Dublin, and normal mastery of northern waters prompted Magnus Barefoot of Norway to make his last great demonstration in 1098. Demonstration is the right word; there was no colonizing stuffing to give it permanent strength.

The results are calculable. There is virtually no significant Scandinavian element in the Welsh language. A few common words which may easily have infiltrated through English – such as *iarll*, the Welsh equivalent of 'earl' – are all that one can point to with certainty. Attempts to suggest that some dialectical changes in the Welsh of the north west or of the south west may be due to Scandinavian influence have not been successful. Neither is there any substantial evidence in favour of institutional change that can properly be attributed to Scandinavian influence, apart perhaps from a certain legal flexibility and willingness to borrow from Anglo-Saxon legal sources prompted in the tenth century by the sheer menace of heathen attack. Very close and careful work on the agrarian structure of medieval Pembrokeshire has failed utterly to disclose anything in the social patterns that can be squared sensibly with the institutions of the Danelaw or the Danicized segments of Normandy. In the last resort the case for Scandinavian settlement in Wales rests on interpretation given to difficult narrative sources and to place-names, supplemented to some extent even by some rather unusual blood-group characteristics discovered by investigations in parts of Pembrokeshire.

Most of the narrative sources, the Lives of the Saints, the Annals and the Anglo-Norman historiography concentrate on dramatic incidents, raids on churches, pillage and rapine, usually by Scandinavians operating well within the Hiberno-Norse circuit. By the end of the eleventh century and the beginning of the twelfth Dublin naval power is an important factor in the general political life of Wales. There is however no explicit reference to Viking settlements in Wales. The most interesting accounts came from later Scandinavian tradition, above all from the *Jomsvikingasaga* which has a series of references to a presumably Danish colony set up in Bretland into which the founder of Jomsborg, Palnatoki, is said to have married. The stories are circumstantial, tell of the establishment of Norsemen in significant numbers even before Palnatoki's first visit (*c.* 930–5), and of the continued existence of the colony throughout the tenth century. We have learned to handle the Jomsvikings with care, and Palnatoki with the utmost scepticism, but there is still interest in the fact that the good twelfth-century storyteller considered that it would not strain the credulity of his readers too far to hear of a Scandinavian kingdom in Wales (always assuming they identified Bretland as Wales). Evidence from place-names and from genealogies is too intangible and has to be forced too hard to make a strong case for associating any specific Viking leader or group with any specific area of Wales. If they did indeed found a more or less permanent settlement in Wales it is likely that it was in the south west around Milford Haven; but beyond that it would be rash to go. Vikings as we know in the Alfredian period moved easily from the South Welsh coast into Devon and Somerset. There are hints of Viking activity of more than mere passing nature in Cornwall. A permanent base in the south-west would have been convenient; but tenth-century equivalents of Waterford or Wexford in Pembrokeshire are no more than hypotheses based on little hard evidence.

The clearest signs of Scandinavian presence in Wales come from place-names, mostly recorded naturally enough in the early stages in English or Latin forms, underlining the complicating factor in all place-name studies that we have so often to take into account the date and language of their first record, both of which can be very different from the date and language of first naming. Things are especially complicated in the Bristol Channel area where the place of first record must often have been the ports, especially Bristol and Dublin rather than the hinterland of the Carmarthenshire or Glamorganshire or Monmouthshire countryside. The vast majority of Scandinavian place-names consist of navigation points and of the names of small islands which themselves could have been previously navigation points. In the north Bardsey (known consistently and unwaveringly in Welsh as Ynys Enlli), Piscar, Holyhead, the Skerries, Priestholm, and Orme's Head fall into this category. Anglesey (consistently Môn in Welsh), meaning Ongull's island, is more difficult to understand. If, as seems certain, it bears the

Scandinavian personal name Ongull there follows a natural assumption that a settlement was made at least on part of the island, presumably at Holyhead, and was in the possession of a Scandinavian community long enough for the name to become current in Chester and Dublin. The name 'Anglesey' is first recorded by the Anglo-Saxon Chronicle in 1098 in connection with Magnus Barefoot's expedition, and twelfth-century belief that both the main Menevian islands, Man and Anglesey, were then known as the islands 'of the English' (*insulae Anglorum*) seems to have been ill-founded. The name 'Anglesey' certainly presents problems, and may suggest at least a temporary establishment of a Scandinavian fortified post in the island. It is unthinkable however that a substantial and enduring colonization took place in this most Welsh of all Welsh communities, *Môn Mam Cymru, Mona,* the mother of Wales.

In the south there is a similar preponderance of navigation point and small island names, again with one or two crucial puzzles. Ramsey, Emsgar, Skomer, Skokholm, Grassholm, Gateholm, Midland (Middelholm) Island, the Tusker Rocks, Stack Rocks, Caldy, Goskar, Burry Holm, Sker, Rothers Sker, and the two holms at the narrow neck of the Channel between East Glamorgan and Somerset, Flat Holm and Steep Holm, fit easily into this category. There are also clusters of names (unfortunately difficult to date precisely) which suggest something more than a sailor's record. In Pembrokeshire Milford Haven (recorded in the late twelfth and early thirteenth centuries as *Milver* and *Mellferth*) is derived from the Scandinavian *fjorðr,* fjord, a good topographical description. Fishguard (*fiskrgarðr* 'fishyard'), Amroth, Colby, Freystrop, Gelliswick, Goultrop, Hasguard, Lydstep, Musselwick and Steynton, all contain probable Scandinavian elements, and some of these places lie inland of the haven. The situation is obscured (as in Ireland) by the Anglo-Norman settlement of Pembroke and the importation of Flemish settlers but there still remains a reasonable case for the physical presence of Scandinavians, colonizing tracts of country behind their main base and navigation centre, the great fjord of Milford. Most but not all (Fishguard itself is a notable exception) apparent Scandinavian settlements lie to the south of the Anglo-Welsh linguistic division which, following the line of early Norman castles from west to east of the shire, is known to this day as the land-share or land-boundary.

Further east than Pembrokeshire there is also some evidence of

Scandinavian influence away from the waters of the Channel. There are Scandinavian names in the princely genealogies of Ystradtawe. Some of the great stone crosses on the Pembrokeshire/Carmarthen border – Nevern and Penally – have marked Scandinavian features. In Glamorgan and especially around Cardiff there are some inland Scandinavian settlement names (Womanby Street in Cardiff (Hundmanby), and Lamby and Homri). But these could be a product of the Anglo-Scandinavian world rather than the Hiberno-Norse: *Hundmanby* is a known form in Yorkshire and the evidence from artistic features would well point to the Danelaw rather than to Ireland. The name Swansea (Sweynesse – probably Sweyn's island) is unquestionably Scandinavian. Worm's Head, on the other hand, is an English form (dragon's head) in contrast to the Norse dragon's head of the north at Orme's Head.

The most that one can do is to try to give a possible interpretation of this difficult evidence in full realization that some of the material may indeed be too ambiguous to bear a heavy weight of synthesis. Coins help us only indirectly since the littoral distribution of coin hoards in Wales is absolute. It is however certain that Scandinavian sailors were active at an early stage in the Bristol Channel and it is quite possible that in the tenth century they set up trading posts in Pembrokeshire and perhaps further east. Indeed one can go further and suggest that they were responsible for the first effective and permanent opening-up of the trading routes from Ireland to Bristol and from Ireland to Chester. They named the navigation points and staging posts in their Scandinavian tongue, and repeated them in that form to the Anglo-Saxon world and to the Anglo-Norman world of 1066–1154. By that time they had probably had an active part to play in the establishment of Bristol and the growth of Chester. There is little evidence of permanent agrarian settlement except, perhaps, in south Pembrokeshire and possibly in and behind Cardiff and Swansea. The great task of the Scandinavians was the concentration on continuous navigation in both principal routes to England from the Irish coast, that is to say, the route to Bristol and the route to Chester; and it is quite possible that they set up their fortified harbours and quays in Milford, in Cardiff and in Swansea as a means of ensuring permanent life to those routes. The most likely period for the realization of permanent settlement of this type could well be the period of relative lull in pirate activity, in the middle years of the tenth century. Progress and development coincided with the rise of Bristol, 990–1040. Agrarian hinterland was of secondary importance even in Pembrokeshire and certainly in Anglesey. Continuous navigation was the aim and the achievement. Such a picture is conjectural but it makes sense. The native Welsh community was relatively untouched except for the disasters to ecclesiastical life that came from occasional raiding. In the north apart from some spill-over into the north east of Wales from the Wirral and Anglo-Scandinavian Cheshire there was no significant agrarian settlement. The Scandinavians were bent on stabilizing routes not on setting up colonies. It is as part of the evolution of the Hiberno-Norse merchant endeavour that Scandinavian impact on Wales must be read.

Further reading

Good detailed bibliographies up to the date of their publication are available in most of the general works mentioned below. Guides to new publications appear annually in *Anglo-Saxon England* (Cambridge University Press). Journals such as *Medieval Archeology* and the *Saga-Book of the Viking Society*, also provide useful means of keeping up with work in progress.

General Works

Gwyn Jones, *A History of the Vikings*, Oxford, 1968, remains an attractive and reliable account. Important insights into the immediate pre-Viking period and given in S. Bassett, *The Origins of Anglo-Saxon Kingdoms*, Leicester, 1989, and *The Age of Sutton Hoo*, ed. Martin Carner, Woodbridge, 1992. Other standard works include:

A. Faulks and R. Perkins (eds), *Viking Revaluations*, Viking Society, London, 1993.

P. G. Foote and D. M. Wilson, *The Viking Achievement*, London, 1970.

J. Graham-Campbell and Dafydd Kidd, *The Vikings*, London, 1980.

J. Graham-Campbell, *The Viking World*, 2nd edn, London, 1990.

F. Donald Logan, *The Vikings in History*, 2nd edn, London, 1991.

Magnus Magnusson, *Viking Expansion Westwards*, London, 1973.

Magnus Magnusson, *Vikings*, London, 1980.

Julian Richards, *Viking Age England*, London, 1991 (strong on archaeology with excellent bibliography).

P. H. Sawyer, *The Age of the Vikings*, 2nd edn, London, 1971.

P. H. Sawyer, *Kings and Vikings*, London, 1982.

D. M. Wilson, *The Vikings and Their Origins: Scandinavia in the first millennium*, London, 1970.

D. M. Wilson, *The Northern World: the history and heritage of Northern Europe, AD 400–1100*, London, 1980.

Proceedings of the Viking Congresses should also be consulted (for example, Tenth Congress, ed. J. E. Knirk, Oslo, 1987).

Works relevant to the chapters of the present book

Chapter 1 The Scandinavian world and Europe in the early Viking Age

The best guides from the European point of view remain Marc Bloch, *Feudal Society*, tr. L. A. Manyon, London, 1961, and the masterly study by Lucien Musset, *Les Invasions: Le Second Assaut contre l' Europe Chrétienne*, Paris, 1965. Other useful guides on specific topics include:

H. R. Ellis Davidson, *Myths and Symbols in Pagan Europe*, Manchester, 1988.
H. H. Lamb, *Climate, Present, Past, and Future*, Vol. 1, London, 1972.
H. R. Loyn and J. Percival, *The Reign of Charlemagne*, London, 1975.
Sean McGrail (ed.), *The Archæology of Medieval Ships and Harbours in Northern Europe*, BAR Supplementary Series, 66, Oxford, 1979.
J. M. Wallace-Hadrill, *The Vikings in Frankia*, Reading, 1975.

Chapters 2 and 3 Britain at the Beginning of the Scandinavian Invasions; The course of the Scandinavian invasions to c.AD 954

Sir Frank Stenton's *Anglo-Saxon England*, 3rd edn, Oxford, 1971, provides an introduction of fundamental importance. Careful attention should also be paid to the mass of original material in translation available in Dorothy Whitelock's *English Historical Documents*, Vol. 1, 2nd edn, London, 1979, and in her edition and translation (with Susie Tucker) of the *Anglo-Saxon Chronicle*, London, 1961. Among many general books *The Anglo-Saxons*, ed. J. Campbell, Oxford, 1982, gives an attractive introduction to the period. Useful studies include:

Martin Biddle and Birth Kjolbye-Biddle, 'Repton and the Vikings', *Antiquity*, 66, 1992.
Barbara Crawford, *Scotland in the Early Middle Ages, Vol. 2: Scandinavian Scotland*, Leicester, 1987.
R. H. M. Dolley (ed.), *Anglo-Saxon Coins*, London, 1961; and *Anglo-Saxon Pennies*, London, 1964.
A. A. M. Duncan, *Scotland, the Making of the Kingdom*, Edinburgh, 1975.
P. Grierson and M. A. S. Blackburn, *Medieval European Coinage*, Cambridge, 1986.
S. D. Keynes and M. Lapidge, *Alfred the Great: Asser's 'Life of King Alfred' and other Contemporary Sources*, London, 1983.

H. R. Loyn, *Anglo-Saxon England and the Norman Conquest*, 2nd edn, London, 1992.

R. I. Page, *An Introduction to English Runes*, London, 1973.

A. P. Symth, *Scandinavian York and Dublin*, two vols, Dublin, 1975–9, and rev. edn, 1987.

A. P. Smyth, *Warlords and Holy Men*, Edinburgh, 1984.

F. T. Wainwright, *The Northern Isles*, London, 1962.

D. Whitelock, 'The conversion of the eastern Danelaw', *Saga-Book of the Viking Society*, London, 1941.

D. M. Wilson, 'Archæological evidence for the Viking settlements and raids in England', *Frühmittelälterliche Studien*, 2, 1968.

Chapters 4 and 5   Scandinavia during the later stages of the Viking Age; The course of the invasions in Britain and Ireland

Many of the studies mentioned in connection with other chapters have relevance here also, but the following books are of direct importance:

K. Randsborg, *The Viking Age in Denmark*, London, 1980.

E. Roesdahl, *Viking Age Denmark*, London, 1982.

E. Roesdahl, *The Vikings*, London, 1991.

P. Sawyer, *Kings and Vikings: Scandinavia and Europe, AD 700–1100*, London, 1982.

P. Sawyer and B. Sawyer, *Medieval Scandinavia*, Minneapolis, 1993.

Other useful studies include:

G. F. Bigelow (ed.), *The Norse of the North Atlantic*, Copenhagen, 1991.

M. A. S. Blackburn and D. M. Metcalf (eds), *Viking-Age Coinage in the Northern Lands*, two parts, BAR Supplementary Series, 122, Oxford, 1981.

C. N. L. Brooke (with Gillian Kerr), *London, 800–1216: the shaping of a city*, London, 1975.

B. G. Charles, *Old Norse Relations with Wales*, Cardiff, 1934.

B. Crawford, 'The pawning of Orkney and Shetland', *Scottish Historical Review*, 48, 1969.

R. A. Hall, *The Excavations at York: the Viking dig*, London, 1984.

Sven Jansson, *Swedish Vikings in England: the evidence of the rune stones*, London, 1966.

M. K. Lawson, *Cnut: the Danes in England in the early eleventh century*, London, 1993.

J. E. Lloyd, *A History of Wales*, two vols, London, 1911.

Magnus Magnusson, *Viking Expansion Westwards*, London, 1973.

D. O'Corrain, *Ireland before the Conquest*, Dublin, 1972.

E. Roesdahl, 'The Danish Geometrical Fortresses and their context', *Anglo-Norman Studies*, 9, ed. R. A. Brown, Woodbridge, 1987.
Dag Strömbäch, *The Conversion of Iceland*, London, 1975.
D. M. Wilson and O. Klindt-Jensen, *Viking Art*, London, 2nd edn, 1980.

Chapter 6 The effects of the Scandinavian invasions on Britain: the problem of settlement

Two valuable collections of essays relating to the general problem of settlement appear in *Medieval Settlement*, ed. P. Sawyer, London, 1976, and *Anglo-Saxon Settlements*, ed. Della Hooke, Oxford, 1988. Controversy over the intensity of Danish settlement in England is best followed in the work of Stenton and Sawyer mentioned above. K. Cameron's analysis of place-names, notably his inaugural lecture 'Scandinavian settlement in the territory of the Five Boroughs', Nottingham, 1966, is fundamental. See also the work of Gillian Fellows-Jensen on place-names and personal names and her shrewd summary 'The Vikings in England: a review', *Anglo-Saxon England*, 4, 1975. Also valuable for their specialist contributions are the following studies:

R. Bailey, *Viking Age Sculpture in Northern England*, London, 1980.
J. R. Baldwin and D. Whyte (eds), *The Scandinavians in Cumbria*, Edinburgh, 1985.
M. A. S. Blackburn (ed.), *Anglo-Saxon Monetary History*, Leicester, 1986.
John Bradley (ed.), *Viking Dublin Exposed: the Wood Quay saga*, Dublin, 1984.
John Bradley (ed.), *Settlement and Society in Medieval Ireland*, Kilkenny, 1988.
K. Cameron, *Place-name Evidence for the Anglo-Saxon Invasion and the Scandinavian Settlements*, English Place-Name Society, Nottingham, 1975.
Barrie Cox, 'Rutland and the Scandinavian settlements: the place-name evidence', *Anglo-Saxon England*, 18, ed. P. Clemoes, 1989.
R. H. M. Dolley, *The Hiberno-Norse Coins in the British Museum*, London, 1966.
Christine Fell et al. (eds), The Viking Age in the Isle of Man, Viking Society for Northern Research, London, 1983.
A. Fenton and H. Palsson (eds), *The Northern and Western Isles in the Viking World: survival, continuity and change*, Edinburgh, 1984.
J. Geipel, *The Viking Legacy. The Scandinavian Influence on the English and Gaelic Languages*, London, 1971.
R. A. Hall, 'The Five Boroughs of the Danelaw: a review of present knowledge', *Anglo-Saxon England*, 18, ed. P. Clemoes, 1989.
K. Hughes, The *Church in Early Irish Society*, London, 1966.

K. Jackson, 'Common Gaelic: the evolution of the Goidelic languages', *Proceedings of the British Academy*, 1951.

K. Jackson, 'The Celtic languages during the Viking period', *Proceedings of the International Congress of Celtic Studies*, 1962.

Otto Jespersen, *Growth and Structure of the English Language*, Oxford, 1935.

H. R. Loyn, *The Vikings in Wales*, London, 1977.

H. R. Loyn, *The Making of the English Nation*, London, 1991.

W. F. H. Nicolaisen, 'Norse settlement in the Northern and Western Isles', *Scottish HR*, 48, 1969.

T. F. O'Rahilly, *Irish Dialects, Past and Present*, Dublin, 1932 (reproduced with improved index, 1972).

R. I. Page, 'How long did the Scandinavian Language survive in England?' *England before the Conquest*, eds P. Clemoes and K. Hughes, Cambridge, 1971.

Melville Richards, 'Norse place-names in Wales', *Proceedings of the International Congress of Celtic Studies*, 1962.

P. Sture Ureland and G. Broderick (eds), *Language Contact in the British Isles*, Max Niemeyer, 1991, especially the essay by John Hines on Old Norse influence in Northumbian English, 403–28.

M. F. Wakelin, *English Dialects: an introduction*, London, 1972.

D. M. Wilson (ed.), *The Archæology of Anglo-Saxon England*, London, 1976.

Index